TWAYNE'S WORLD AUTHORS SERIES

A Survey of the World's Literature

Sylvia E. Bowman, Indiana University

GENERAL EDITOR

FRANCE

Maxwell A. Smith, Guerry Professor of French, Emeritus

The University of Chattanooga

Visiting Professor in Modern Languages

The Florida State University

EDITOR

Georges Bernanos

(T W A S 71)

TWAYNE'S WORLD AUTHORS SERIES (TWAS)

The purpose of TWAS is to survey the major writers —novelists, dramatists, historians, poets, philosophers, and critics—of the nations of the world. Among the national literatures covered are those of Australia, Canada, China, Eastern Europe, France, Germany, Greece, India, Italy, Japan, Latin America, New Zealand, Poland, Russia, Scandinavia, Spain, and the African nations, as well as Hebrew, Yiddish, and Latin Classical literatures. This survey is complemented by Twayne's United States Authors Series and English Authors Series.

The intent of each volume in these series is to present a critical-analytical study of the works of the writer; to include biographical and historical material that may be necessary for understanding, appreciation, and critical appraisal of the writer; and to present all material in clear, concise English—but not to vitiate the scholarly content of the work by doing so.

Georges Bernanos

By WILLIAM BUSH
University of Western Ontario

Twayne Publishers, Inc.   : :   New York

MANUFACTURED IN THE UNITED STATES OF AMERICA

Preface

In keeping with Twayne Publishers' policy of producing volumes on single authors designed to serve "a general reader, college teachers and students, high school teachers and students," I have tried, in writing this study of Bernanos, to bear in mind the importance of a general presentation of the man and his work rather than a presentation concentrating primarily on the many interpretations possible for a difficult novel such as *M. Ouine*. The biographical section has, moreover, been written so that it may serve, in its own right, as a short introduction to Bernanos.

The largest portion of the text, the discussion of Bernanos' fiction, has been constructed so as to lead the uninitiated reader into that unusual and difficult literary world as painlessly as possible. This discussion will open with a general survey of the author's whole artistic vision before attempting the summary of his novels and a specialized analysis of each. Thus, it is hoped, the reader will, from the beginning, become intrigued by Bernanos' whole literary world. This would be impossible if the reader were to begin by plunging into the darksome shades of Bernanos' first novel, *Under the Sun of Satan*.

Because of the singular ties between Bernanos' life and the complex chronology of his novels, details concerning this interplay are necessarily considered in both the biographical section and in the section on the novels. This double treatment of certain crucial details should not, however, in any way disconcert either the general reader or the specialist; rather it will put into better perspective the basic known facts involved in Bernanos' evolution as a writer.

One liberty has been taken in regard to the publisher's policy of using translated titles of books where such exist. Bernanos' difficult "great novel," *M. Ouine*, is referred to throughout as *M. Ouine* and not as *The Open Mind* since this translation, now out of print, proved so highly unsatisfactory that, very probably, it will not be reprinted. A similar policy could have applied in the similar case of *Dialogues des Carmélites*, whose first rendering into English as *The Fearless Heart* proved equally unsatisfactory. A more recent translation, entitled *The Carmelites*, is now available, however, and so this latter title has been used throughout. In the case of *Sous le Soleil de Satan*, I have chosen Harry Lorin Binsse's title *Under the Sun of Satan*. Anne Green's translation of *Un Crime* was entitled *The Crime* in England, *A Crime* in America; I have used the American title.

I have written this volume after fifteen years of relative intimacy with the work of Georges Bernanos. To name all who during these fifteen years have aided me as I tried to grasp that vast dream which dominated the work of this author and which so often had direct bearing on his life, would be impossible. My gratitude to all who have shared with me their own rich store of personal memories and reflections can hardly be expressed since a certain modesty imposes itself when one shares the secrets of a great love.

More immediately, however, there are those who were specifically connected with this particular work. First, my cordial thanks to my former colleague and faithful friend, Dr. Thomas Cordle, of Duke University, who was directly responsible for my being given the opportunity to write the Twayne volume on Bernanos. The Duke University Council on Research generously supported this project by awarding me a Summer Research Fellowship for 1965 and by further assisting me in returning to France with a travel grant during my sabbatical leave in 1965–66. In Canada I am indebted to Dean R. N. Shervill of Middlesex College, the University of Western Ontario, for the awarding of a Middlesex College Research Grant for 1966–67 as well as for the extraordinary assistance afforded me by the Middlesex College Stenographic Pool. There the expertise and patience of Mrs. A. Marshall alone was responsible for rendering an illegible manuscript into a final draft and fair copy. To my departmental chairman and old friend, Dr. Weston Flint, and to his secretary, Miss Kathleen Walker, my sincerest thanks for their constant cooperation and sympathetic understanding.

Preface

Finally, I am particularly indebted to Sister Meredith Murray, O.P., of Rosary College, for her friendship and invaluable aid. One can but stand in admiration of the vital store of biographical detail which she has so painstakingly amassed as she prepares the forthcoming edition of Bernanos' correspondence, a work very eagerly awaited by all interested in Bernanos. It is also imperative that I give a word of affectionate recognition to my long-suffering spouse whose judgment I so constantly rely upon and refer to as I write.

WILLIAM BUSH

London, Canada
June, 1967

Contents

GEORGES BERNANOS

by

WILLIAM BUSH

Since his death in 1948 Georges Bernanos has been increasingly regarded with profound respect by students of French literature. The inimitable author of *Sous le Soleil de Satan* and *Journal d'un Curé de Campagne* now appears to have been granted a place among the few truly notable authors of the first half of the 20th century.

For a number of reasons, however, Bernanos has not enjoyed as universal a reception among English-language readers as have his co-religionists, Claudel and Mauriac. The present volume aims at presenting to non-French readers the contemporary relevance of Bernanos' work and thought, giving particular emphasis to the complex and highly personal genesis of his nine volumes of fiction.

Writing primarily for readers totally unfamiliar with the author of *Dialogues des Carmélites* and *M. Ouine*, Professor Bush gives an introduction to the interior life of the man and the aesthetic and spiritual evolution of the writer, drawing upon a long familiarity with Bernanos' work and thought as well as upon friendship with many who were his intimates.

Chronology

1888   Born Georges Bernanos on February 20 in Paris, the son of Emile, an interior decorator and furnisher, and of Hermance (*née* Moreau), at 26, rue Joubert.

1898   Enters Parisian Jesuit *collège*, rue de Vaugirard, as day student. First Communion there on May 11, 1899.

1901   Jesuit *collège* closed, Bernanos transferred to Petit-Séminaire of Notre-Dame-des-Champs as boarding student.

1903   Unable to adjust to Parisian boarding school life, he is sent to the provinces to the Petit Séminaire of Saint-Célestin at Bourges.

1904   Failing his first *baccalauréat*, he is transferred to yet another provincial school, Collège Sainte-Marie at Aire-sur-Lys, near the family's country home at Fressin.

1905   His first *baccalauréat* passed, he proceeds to the second one. A passionate partisan of the rising royalist movement. Devours the works of Balzac, Hello, Barbey, Zola, Sir Walter Scott and Drumont.

1906   The second *"bachot"* completed, he undertakes university studies in Paris at the Faculty of Law and the Institut Catholique, preparing a *licence* in law and letters.

1907   First efforts at fiction published in small royalist paper.

1908   *Action française* launches daily newspaper.

1909   *Camelots du Roi* organized by *Action française* and Bernanos soon heads a small, noisy group of *camelots*. Troubles with police and brief imprisonment resulting from demonstrations.

1911	Brief stint of military service in the Sixth Dragoons. Unable to continue for reasons of health, he is deferred to return to studies.
1913–1914	His studies finished and two degrees completed, he takes job as editor of small royalist weekly at Rouen, *L'Avant-Garde de Normandie*. Three early short stories published in this paper.
1914	With outbreak of war, he gets himself accepted again in the Sixth Dragoons where he will fight throughout the war, will be wounded and decorated.
1917	Dramatic encounter with work of Léon Bloy during period of convalescence. On May 11 marries Jeanne Talbert d'Arc at Vincennes. Léon Daudet is best man, Dom Besse officiant.
1918	Birth of first child. By 1933 there will be six.
1919	Introduced to Robert Vallery-Radot by Dom Besse. Works as insurance inspector, traveling in eastern France, writing his first novel on trains and in cafés.
1922	Short story "Madame Dargent" appears in *Revue hebdomadaire*.
1923	Grave illness. Does not want to die "without having witnessed." Family pilgrimage to Lourdes.
1924	Moves from Paris to Bar-le-Duc to be nearer work.
1925	*Under the Sun of Satan* finished and entrusted to Valley-Radot.
1926	*Under the Sun of Satan* immediate and unexpected success. He abandons his job in order to write. Begins second novel, *L'Imposture*. *Action française* condemned by Pope.
1927	Death of father. Pilgrimage to Lourdes. First refuses *Légion d'Honneur*. Finishes *L'Imposture*. Buys large house at Clemont-de-l'Oise and starts *Joy*. *L'Imposture* published in October.
1928	Pilgrimages to La Salette and Ars. Begins "biography" of Drumont. *Joy* finished in December.
1929	*Joy* published in April, receives *Prix Fémina* in December. Bernanos supports *Action française*.

1930	Death of mother. Treated for nervous condition during summer. Completes book on Drumont, *La Grande peur des bien-pensants*. Moves to southern coast.
1931	In January begins *Night Is Darkest*, then *M. Ouine* in February. *La Grande peur* appears in April. In July, family installed in large villa at La Bayorre. Finances become problem. Articles undertaken for *Le Figaro*.
1932	May–November violent polemic between *Action française* and Bernanos. He returns to work on *M. Ouine*.
1933	*M. Ouine* interrupted by motorcycle accident in July which leaves Bernanos crippled for life. Birth of sixth child in September. Financial crisis mounting. He returns desperately to *M. Ouine*.
1934	First thirteen chapters of *M. Ouine* sent to Plon in March. Detective story, *A Crime*, undertaken for money. Contract signed with Plon for advanced royalties to be paid on each page of manuscript sent them. As final act of desperation, family leaves La Bayorre, sailing for Majorca and cheaper living, abandoning books and furniture to an impatient landlord. *Diary of a Country Priest* begun in December.
1935	*A Crime* finished; appears in July. *Night Is Darkest* completed in July, stuck away in drawer.
1936	*The Diary of a Country Priest*, published in March, receives *Grand Prix du Roman* of the French Academy. Spanish Civil War. *Mouchette* begun.
1937	Return to France's southern coast. Rewrites book on Spanish Civil War, having lost first manuscript. *Mouchette* published in May.
1938	*Les Grands cimetières sous la lune* published in May. Refuses *Légion d'Honneur* for second time. Embarkation in July with family for Paraguay, whence they move on to Brazil.
1939	*Scandale de la vérité* completed in January. At Vas-

souras he completes *Nous autres Français* in June. In September undertakes raising cattle on great estate near Pirapora. *Les Enfants humiliés* begun.

1940   *Les Enfants humiliés* completed, also last chapter of *M. Ouine*. Moves to small farm at Barbecena where he will remain four years.

1942–1944   Uses pen to support Free French and the Resistance. *Plea for Liberty* published in Rio de Janeiro in 1942, secretly circulated in Europe as will also be articles collected under title *Le Chemin de la Croix-des-Ames* and, in 1944, *La France contre les robots*. *M. Ouine* published in Rio de Janeiro in 1943.

1945   The war over, General de Gaulle sends for Bernanos who hesitatingly accepts after the third appeal, returning in July.

1945–1947   Forever restless, he moves south from Paris, writing newspaper articles and giving lectures. Third refusal of *Légion d'Honneur* in 1946, the year *M. Ouine* is published in France for the first time, using the faulty text from Rio de Janeiro.

1947   Leaves France for last time for Tunisia, settling first at Hammamet, then at Gabbès. During last winter writes *The Carmelites*, his first fiction since 1940.

1948   *The Carmelites* completed, Bernanos takes to his bed for the last time. Flown back to Paris for an operation, his last six weeks are spent in the American Hospital where he dies on the morning of July 5. Interred at Pellevoisin.

1949   Albert Béguin, Bernanos' literary executor, publishes *The Carmelites* and launches the Société des Amis de Georges Bernanos.

1950   Béguin publishes *Night Is Darkest* with Plon.

1951   Béguin publishes essay on Luther in *Esprit*.

1953   *Last Essays* prepared for publication by Béguin and published by Gallimard.

1955   Béguin brings out first integral edition of *M. Ouine*.

1956   Early essays published by Gallimard as *Le Crépu-*
        scule des vieux.

1957   *The Carmelites* set to music by Francis Poulenc and
        performed at La Scala in Milan. Death of Albert
        Béguin.

1961   Bernanos' post-war articles published by Gallimard
        as *Français, si vous saviez.*

1962   Pléiade edition of Bernanos' *Oeuvres romanesques,*
        using integral text of Béguin for *M. Ouine.*

Part I

The Man

ON July 5, 1948, as the first rays of dawn appeared outside the window of a room of the American Hospital in the fashionable Parisian suburb of Neuilly-sur-Seine, Georges Bernanos, lying in a bed for which he himself could not afford to pay, succumbed to an infection of the liver. The vigil had been long for his family, friends and the young curé of Saint-Séverin who had attended him. Six weeks before, a devoted wealthy friend had had the author flown from Tunisia to the Paris Hospital for an operation in which no one really believed. But Paris, where Bernanos was born on February 20, 1888, now at his death, sixty years later, claimed him again as her own.

Many times Paris had provided the scene for Bernanos' tempestuous, errant life. He gained a great part of his early education there, and his entire higher education. It was in Paris during those stormy years of 1908–1913 that *Action française,* the daily newspaper of the monarchist movement headed by Charles Maurras, spurred students such as he to violent attacks on all that the Third Republic stood for. And, even if it was in Rouen that Bernanos would find his wife, they began their life together after World War I in the capital. Though they moved briefly from Paris to Bernanos' ancestral Lorraine for a year, the writer's literary success immediately brought him back again to the city of his birth.

Had Bernanos been capable of becoming the usual man of letters and had his wife's health not dictated their living in a more southern climate, the remainder of his life might well have been spent in Paris in quiet, modest comfort. But success was brief, and failure followed mercilessly. There followed, too, an almost nomadic search for peace and security for the great, tormented spirit of this unusual man.

If a book should some day be written on Bernanos' different residences, it will carry its writer far. From France's Belgian border on the north to the Mediterranean coast on the south, from the Spanish island of Majorca to the jungle forests of Brazil, from North Africa back to Paris, such is the itinerary one would be obliged to follow. For Bernanos' spirit was restless, and this restlessness was undoubtedly closely tied to his inability to organize his family life. The first of his six children was born in 1919, the last in 1933; the relentless demands of growing hungry children and an ailing exhausted wife formed the excruciating, familiar background against which he would write five of his eight novels. Yet in these novels Bernanos always sought, even in the depths of evil, how best to articulate his vision of "God's sweet mercy."

After God, however, France was Bernanos' greatest obsession. He finally even sacrificed writing novels in order to write for France during the war. This deliberate action on his part has left the world some of the most remarkable pages written during World War II on European civilization, on man and his destiny. Bernanos' non-fiction is, in fact, more considerable in volume than his fiction. Yet the depth he achieves in his nine volumes of fiction (including his eight novels plus *The Carmelites*) and the impact these books are still capable of producing on the reader will cause him to be remembered in the literary world primarily for his imaginative work.

Yet, after the four-month period represented by February–May, 1940, when Bernanos, having abandoned his "masterpiece" *M. Ouine* four years before, returned to write the last chapter of that novel even as France fell to the enemy, the author was never again to write another novel. Indeed, the only fiction he would ever write again would be the dialogues for a screen scenario, *The Carmelites,* finished just before his death.

There is thus a certain enigma to Bernanos as a novelist just as there are many enigmas to him as a man. And that he should be brought to an elegant Parisian suburb to die in a hospital identified with a nation on whose soil he had refused to set foot is strangely ironical. His requiem in Saint-Séverin in that Latin Quarter where he had given rein to his youthful violences, the absence at that ceremony of any major literary figure except for the faithful, nonbelieving André Malraux, the pall of silence which surrounded his work in the late forties and early fifties, and the recent naming of a Paris street after him, located where he himself had once animated the youth of the *Action française*—all these coincidences seem to partake of the inexplicable mystery which surrounds him who has been called—whatever it may mean—the "French Dostoyevsky."

Indeed, the element of mystery is very strong in both Bernanos' life and works. For the reader who desires books devoid of this element of mystery it is undoubtedly best to bypass the works of Bernanos. But Bernanos' knowledge of man's inexplicable nature is rare and, for those seeking an honest explanation of the true human situation, the author's entire work will be rich in appeal.

Whether exploring the black light of Satan's sun in the heart of man or the terrifying implication of Christian joy, whether following human torment in liars, drug addicts and seducers or the transfiguring Christian acceptation of existence which can but lead to the world's scaffolds, there is an inviolable element of mystery present. This element will inevitably leave the reader ill at ease; but, just as inevitably, the reader will be much the wiser and more discerning of man's misery and greatness as, led by Bernanos, he struggles to understand "God's sweet mercy."

I Family Background

Some ground exists for supposing a very distant Spanish origin for Bernanos' name. As early as 1298, Spanish settlers were actually to be found in the Trois-Evêchés region of Lorraine to which the writer's ancestors have been traced.[1] The Spanish side of Bernanos, however, remarked upon from time to time by literary critics to explain his fervent faith and his violent condemnation of modern civilization, would actually appear to be due largely to individual temperament rather than to blood, since the possibility of direct Spanish influence is very far removed.

The hispanic appearance of the name, however, did give rise within Bernanos' family itself to a legend which linked it to a pirate adventurer of that name in Santo-Domingo during the Spanish colonialization of the new world. Yet careful research has shown that this family legend is without historical foundation since the true ancestors of the writer, the "Burnanos" family, were already established in France near Metz, at Ancy-sur-Moselle in Lorraine, in the mid-sixteenth century.[2]

From Ancy-sur-Moselle the Bernanos family moved into Metz. Then, by the end of the eighteenth century, they had settled at Bouzonville, still in the same region. These moves were accompanied by advances in social milieux as they moved from agriculture into business and bourgeois life. It has even been established, for the delight of those numerous readers of Bernanos who insist on seeing in him, first and last, "the novelist of the priest," that there was one cleric in the family at the beginning of the eighteenth century: Nicholas Bernanos, curé of Varize.[3]

In 1852, in keeping with the Industrial Revolution's general effect of uprooting, the writer's paternal grandfather, a cobbler, left the ancestral Lorraine, taking the train for Paris. He installed himself in the suburbs of the capital at La Villette and, according to the declaration of birth when Bernanos' father was born, worked as a day laborer.[4]

Though equally rooted in French soil, the writer's maternal origins were hardly more exalted by worldly standards. Born in the province of Berry in central France of peasants who had left the land and moved into the small town of Pellevoisin, Bernanos' mother came to Paris in service to a great lady. When the girl decided to marry Emile Bernanos, her mistress accorded her a dowry which was to assist the young husband in launching himself in business.[5] Thus, thanks to his mother's good fortune and his father's business ability, the future writer was destined to be the son of a solid bourgeois interior decorater and dealer in interior furnishings. This worldly prosperity would inevitably affect the whole formation of the Bernanos' only son.

Of great importance to any literary study of Bernanos is the fact that his father's success in the capital enabled the family to purchase a huge country house in northern France in the wooded region of Artois. Located in the tiny village of Fressin in the administrative *département* of Pas-de-Calais, the original house, destroyed by fire during the last war, was quite close to the site of the famed battle of Agincourt. This part of France, so near the seacoast, is frequently drenched in rain and mist. The sea wind and clouds roll in from the Atlantic, sweep through the lush greenery and lend a savage wildness to what might otherwise be a very tranquil spot of luxuriant natural beauty. The author's fidelity to his memories of Artois, revealed in novels he wrote after the house had passed from his family's hands in 1925, reveals the depth of that indelible imprint left on him by his childhood stays there.

II *Childhood: 1888–1899*

To Emile and Hermance Bernanos was born, in 1883, their first child and only daughter, the writer's sister Thérèse. Georges, their second and last child, was born five years later on February 20, 1888, at 26, rue Joubert, at that time also the address of his father's business. The family later moved to 14, rue Vignon, but by 1899 were installed at 82, rue Abbé-Groult.

One gathers from remarks made by Bernanos in subsequent years that a number of parental dispositions were to mark him for life. In spite of the fact that such outstanding Catholic theologians as Hans Urs von Balthazar and Yves Congar have devoted studies to Bernanos' work, the author himself always disclaimed any knowledge of formal theology: he knew only what he had learned in his catechism at his mother's knee. His mother's influence, then, would appear to have been the instillation in him of that traditional French piety which has its roots in centuries of Christian orientation towards life. The belief that the future writer was miraculously cured as a small child by the intercession of Our Lady of Victories[6] was thus as much a part of daily life as was the fact that he had been born.

The father's influence, however, would appear to have been of a more active, less contemplative sort. He maintained an impressive library at the country house at Fressin and was a regular reader of *La Libre Parole*. Published by the arch anti-Semite, Edouard Drumont, this daily newspaper aimed at alerting Frenchmen to the dangers of international Jewry, allegedly then in the process of taking over France. In those years of the Dreyfus affair, the greatest danger, as Drumont saw it, was the loss of France's basic hierarchy of values, a hierarchy respected during all those centuries since France had first been converted to Christianity. That hierarchy of values which had made France's history one of grandeur and glory, Bernanos was later to remind his readers, was not based on money.

Drumont's incessant exposure of fraud and intrigue, as he tried to prove that France was being undermined, nurtured the young boy's sense of revolt at a world which would allow such injustice. At least one of Bernanos' books is directly connected to his father's reading habits. Had Emile Bernanos read a less radical paper, one more in sympathy with government of the Third Republic than *La Libre Parole* of Drumont, Bernanos might never have written his book on Drumont, *La Grande peur des bienpensants.*

It is important to underline the fact that the Bernanos household, even though the parents had evolved socially and economically from peasant and working-class backgrounds, was still, indeed, strongly tied to those old values in which French honor came second only to God. Bernanos was thus reared in an atmosphere where people were aware of their Christian past as well as their national past. He was always to remain faithful both to Christianity and to the monarchist ideal, in spite of the conflicts he had with those who might, from time to time, set themselves up as official spokesmen for both the Church and pretender: the Jesuits and Charles Maurras. Never, however, was Bernanos to flinch in his allegiance either to God or to the historic house of France.

Of equal importance in the family household, however, was the spirit of freedom, of open, free criticism of all that appeared unjust, whether found in the Church or in monarchist politics. To this spirit of freedom Bernanos also remained faithful throughout his life, disregarding all possibly unhappy consequences of such a stand.

At the end of his life, in an address he gave to a group of nuns in 1947,[7] the year before his death, the author raised freedom to the highest theological and metaphysical level. In this address Bernanos maintains that since God had made his creation free, giving man the scandalous choice of not loving Him, there must be freedom for man to live both as a man and as a Christian. Bernanos faced the terrible responsibility of freedom in full acknowledgment of the fact that evil itself had come into the world from this scandalous gift of freedom. Yet he insisted that without freedom there can be no love: love is dependent upon a free choice not to love. For Bernanos, the protection of man's freedom, so that man can thereby opt to love, is the modern world's fundamental battle on both a spiritual and a material plane.

The ideal of freedom to think, to reflect, to criticize and to love, learned in his childhood at the family table, thus carried over into Bernanos' adult life and to this ideal he was to cling faithfully to the end. He told all those who, he thought, endangered freedom that they were committing treason to the human race and acting for the demonic forces which aim at perverting God's purpose in creating man to love.

III *Education: 1899–1906*

By the time his son was ten years old, Emile Bernanos was able to send him to one of the most esteemed schools for boys in Paris, the *collège* run by the Jesuits on rue de Vaugirard. Among the future writer's fellow students at the Jesuit college was another destined for glory: Charles de Gaulle.

As a day student in the school, young Georges was here prepared for his first Communion, which he received on May 11, 1899, at the age of eleven. This unique experience so deeply moved the young adolescent that he still recalled it even on his deathbed. In his prayers of thanksgiving to God, after receiving the holy sacrament for the first time, he asked for one single gift: the grace to become a missionary.

Bernanos remained as a day student with the Jesuits until the *collège* closed down in 1901 when the law against religious congregations was passed. Although the enforcement of the law was to come slightly later, the Jesuits were aware that even if other orders might possibly receive government permission to continue operation, they themselves were certain to be evicted. During these three very crucial and formative years, from 10 to 13, Bernanos seems to have formed friendship which would be lifelong with Guy de Bouteiller and Ernest de Malibran.

With the closing of this establishment, the boy was transferred to another school, the Petit Séminaire of Notre-Dame-des-Champs, this time as a boarder. To his old friends from the Jesuit college who were also transferred to Notre-Dame-des-Champs he now added another: Maxence de Colleville to whom he would dedicate *La Grande peur des bien-pensants* and for whose brother, Yves, killed in World War I, Bernanos would name his eldest son.

Apart from these friendships, the two years spent at Notre-Dame-des-Champs, 1901–1903, were seemingly a failure. Reflecting upon these days in a boarding school run by a Jesuit superior, Bernanos was later to recall them as a "real panic," finding the system used there as apparently constructed only to find fault and create a bad conscience.[8] It is not surprising, therefore, that the Jesuit superior of the institution finally recommended to the boy's parents that they transfer him to a commercial school. The parents, however, did not follow this well-meant recommendation.

It is of interest to note that Bernanos was, in spite of difficulties in his education, already a reader. He avows to have read the complete works of Balzac in his father's library, to which he had stolen the key, at the age of thirteen. Furthermore, after the publication of his first novel it was Balzac's name which immediately came to the fore when Bernanos was queried about literary influences. Although he claimed never to have re-read the master's works for fear of being disappointed, we are told by one of his teachers that he was still reading Balzac at age sixteen and must have re-read him many times. We know, too, that the works of Sir Walter Scott excited his enthusiasm during these years when he is also believed to have read Barbey d'Aurevilly, the one novelist who can clearly be cited as a direct forerunner of Bernanos as a novelist.

In the face of their failure at the Parisian school, the Bernanos parents now turned to acquaintances for help. During the boy's last two years at the Jesuit college, 1899–1901, a weekly visitor to the Bernanos household was a young priest, Abbé Signargout, from Madame Bernanos' native province of Berry, who was preparing his *licence* in Paris.[9] He was frequently accompanied by his friend, also from Berry, Abbé Lagrange. Both these young priest-teachers had now completed their *licence* and had returned to Berry where they were teaching at the Petit Séminaire Saint-Célestin at Bourges. Thus, in 1903, on the advice of Abbé Signargout, it was decided to send the fifteen-year-old Georges to the *collège* in his mother's native province.

It was undoubtedly assumed that Georges would complete his

secondary education there; yet, as will be seen, his stay at Saint-Célestin was to be limited to only one year. Nonetheless, during that year there was a seeming change for the better: the boy's morale had improved and he had formed a very close tie with Abbé Lagrange, his teacher of rhetoric.

French secondary education, the same in both the state-supported *lycée* and the private *collège,* terminates with the passing of the second *baccalauréat,* the diploma necessary for admission to university. If all had progressed normally, sixteen-year-old Georges would have passed the first of these at the end of his year at Saint-Célestin. Having failed to do so, he prepared for the "second try" examination given in the fall before the new year. Failing again, he would now be obliged to repeat the year he had just completed.

The boy's parents sought the advice of the curé of Fressin. He it was who suggested a nearby *collège,* Sainte-Marie, at Aire-sur-Lys where a number of army families stationed in the vicinity sent their sons to mix with the provincial students of the institution. Here, from 1904–1906, the teenager completed his secondary studies, passing his first *baccalauréat* in 1905 and the second one in 1906.

These years are some of the best documented for the reader today, thanks to the letters Bernanos wrote back to Abbé Lagrange at Saint-Célestin.[10] The Bernanos parents had invited Abbé Lagrange to spend a summer holiday at Fressin in 1904 while Georges was preparing his "second try" examination for the first *baccalauréat.* The letters which the boy wrote his friend throughout the two succeeding years open many perspectives on the state of his interior life and his deepest preoccupations and aspirations during that time.

The boy's preoccupation with death, his fear that the slightest illness would be fatal to him, was balanced by an unusually well-formed conviction about the importance of the place accorded God in one's life. God must be mixed into everything, he maintained. Morover, one can detect Bernanos' thirst for God alone in his observation that all that is not God does not satisfy. Of interest also are his rejection of all sentimentality and his fear of being weakened in his convictions by it. The fact that he had an extraordinarily sympathetic heart, the heart of the most sensitive poet,

and yet was determined so to discipline it that in no way could
he be led by its passions provides an important insight into the
writer's personal and interior struggle. It provides as well a
glimpse of one of the forces behind his novels' greatness.

From conversations with both a professor and a fellow student
of Bernanos' during these last two years of his secondary education at Aire-sur-Lys[11] it can be gathered that he held himself
somewhat aloof from his provincial classmates and, to a certain
degree, posed as the sophisticated Parisian. One of his classmates,
in 1957 a venerable village curé who had spent his life in that
same region, remarked to the present writer: "He never came
back for any of the reunions." Yet this same curé still remembered the Christmas party when Bernanos, treasurer of the local
chapter of the Society of St. Vincent de Paul, got up on the stage
and made a very good speech. It would appear from this that he
did not divorce himself from all the good works of the country
school. Bernanos' professor of French at this period also had
some interesting comments to make fifty years later—also in
1957. He recalled his former student's liking for Zola as well as
his ardent royalist sympathies.

At this collège, besides successfully completing his two bacca-
lauréats, Bernanos also found a good spiritual director who
introduced him to the works of Ernest Hello, a fitting contrast to
the naturalist novels of Zola. The works of Hello, virtually un-
heard of even in English-speaking countries, deal with very lofty
aspects of God's glory and of man's vocation to it—two preoccupations which also were to remain with Bernanos until the end.

In 1906, after Bernanos had passed the second baccalauréat,
Abbé Lagrange was again invited to spend his summer holiday
at Fressin. This visit was, however, to end his rapports with the
maturing boy. A bit more speculative than his former student on
the subject of the Church's social obligations, the priest could
not see how his young friend preferred to scorn Marc Sangnier's
Catholic democratic Sillon movement in favor of the more militant royalist movement, Action française. Master of this royalist
movement was the agnostic poet, publicist and political thinker,
Charles Maurras, a man steeped in the pagan glories of Greece
and Rome. Yet the Action française would claim Bernanos' sympathy as well as provide a carnal reality for his monarchist ideal-

ism until his dramatic and painful public break with Maurras in 1932. The *Action française* was also to be at the center of Bernanos' extracurricular activities during those university days in Paris which now were upon him.

IV *University Days: 1906–1913*

Entering upon university studies in 1906 at the faculty of Law and at the Institut Catholique, Bernanos by 1913 had completed two degrees: a *licence* in letters and one in law. Then, in the ten months immediately preceding the outbreak of the World War I, he would actually embark upon a brief career as the editor of a small royalist newspaper in Rouen. But the seven years in Paris which prepared Bernanos for this brief accolade of official royalist glory must have caused him to smile indulgently in later years as he summed it all up in the words "I loved noise!"

In 1906 there was nothing at all surprising that Bernanos, given his family background, should rally around those who advocated overthrowing the Third Republic "by all means—even legal ones." He was in the forefront of demonstrations and street fights and even spent a few days in the *Santé* prison in 1909, at a moment when the royalist students were storming the weekly lecture of Thalamas. Thalamas was a professor lecturing at the Sorbonne who, five years earlier at the Lycée Condorcet, was reputed to have insulted Joan of Arc, the patroness of the young royalists and the symbol of all that was most purely and most nobly Christian and French. Bernanos' first literary attempts were also made at this period and were published by a small royalist review as early as 1907.

Joining up with de Malibran, de Colleville and de Bouteiller, his old friends from his days at Notre-Dame-des-Champs, Bernanos found in them enthusiastic support for his own royalist views and emerged as the leader of their small group. They called themselves the "Men of War," and "War" was not too much of an exaggeration of terms since the *Action française* movement had become powerful enough to start publishing a daily newspaper in 1908. In the public announcement launching the newspaper on March 21, 1908, readers were reminded:

The republic is evil itself; the republic is Jewish government; the republic is government of Protestant pedagogues; the republic is government of Freemasons; the republic is government of those more or less naturalized foreigners, or *métèques* who these days are soiling the disaffected Panthéon with the cadaver of their Zola.

Demonstrations in the Latin Quarter broke out two months later, in May, showing that the Royalists-Nationalists had considerable strength among the students. By November of the same year, just when the various university faculties would be getting under way, there was an open appeal in the paper for "voluntary hawkers" (*Camelots volontaires*) to sell the newspaper "in the streets and especially at the doors of churches." Thus evolved a sizeable and militant group of young men who took the name "The King's Hawkers" (*Les Camelots du Roi*).

The young supporters of Marc Sangnier's *Sillon* movement also hawked papers in front of churches, but they were viewed as representatives of the hated enemy. Clashes with them as well as with other more numerous—and less Christian—non-royalists prompted the "King's Hawkers" to organize a body of guards to protect those who did the actual "hawking." From this beginning was to evolve the image of that aggressive royalist guard which is usually associated with the mention of the *Camelots du Roi*. D. W. Brogan even goes so far as to see in the *Camelots du Roi* a very tiny prefiguration of Hitler's storm troopers.[12] In spite of a certain accuracy in this observation (both groups found in the nationalistic idealism of young enthusiasts their major appeal; in the World War II the *Action française* was accused of collaboration with the Nazis, and Maurras himself died in prison after being convicted of collaboration), the young of any country and of any generation can, after all, be whipped into militant, violent patriotism.

That the *Action française* expanded into publishing its own daily newspaper in 1908 is an indication of the political feeling of the time. In 1899, Captain Dreyfus had been pardoned and in 1906 he was restored to full military status. Those who had been against Dreyfus had found in *La Libre Parole* of Edouard Drumont their daily reminder that there was no justice in the world: the forces of international, rootless Jewry had joined with those of French Protestants and Freemasons and the hated foreigners living in France to spoil the last vestiges of Christian France through their lust for money and personal interests. And so they turned in large part to Maurras and his movement for encouragement that all was not yet lost for their noble and historically founded cause.

The newspaper *Action française,* quick to exploit the existence of the *Camelots* and to spur them on to greater violence, provided the young men Maurice Pujo, Maurras' personal representative, who served as mentor for attacks on such venerable institutions as the Sorbonne and the *Comédie française.* The chief of the *Camelots* was a student of sculpture at the *Ecole des Beaux-Arts* with the imposing name of Maxime Real del Sarte who found it as easy to get himself arrested twice in the same day as to slap a professor at the Sorbonne before his students.

Bernanos' "Men of War" were all inscribed in the *Camelots,* and Bernanos himself was convicted of "disturbing the peace" by shouting slogans. He also had the enviable glory of being wounded in battle and of being fêted at one of the numerous dinners honoring the royalist heroes.

However, all was not absolutely tranquil between Bernanos and *Action française* officialdom even during these days. There are indications of Bernanos' independence from Pujo and Maurras, for on one occasion Bernanos lent his support and that of his "Men of War" to an ill-fated attempt to take the boat for Portugal to aid in restoring the king who had been overthrown there by the revolution in October, 1910.

When word of the affair got out before the departure, Bernanos was summoned before the *Action française* "War Council" presided over by Pujo and the dowager patroness of the movement. This great lady, Madame la Marquise de MacMahon, was the maternal guardian angel of the *Camelots* and is reported to have cried "I love violence" at one of the heroes' dinners staged by the *Action française* to honor the wounded or imprisoned *Camelots.* In spite of the Marquise's august presence, however, Bernanos refused to submit to Pujo's insistence that party doctrine came first. In Bernanos' mind, the King of Portugal was also a king, and Christian honor was Christian honor, regardless of where it was encountered.

In 1911, Bernanos began his required stint of military service.
His health, however, never very robust, could not take the strain,
and he was deferred after a short period of service with the Sixth
Regiment of Dragoons at Evreux. He returned to Paris and the
freer militarism of the *Camelots*. In 1912 he was wounded when
the *Camelots* invaded a meeting of Bonapartists. Again, when
the Sorbonne gathered to honor Rousseau, Bernanos was among
those interrupting the event.[13]

Yet these days were also filled with contacts with the reality
of the lower classes. Through Cercle Proudhon upper-class students met with young workers to discuss mutual action to save
France from her exploiters, those who had interest only in money
and personal advantage. A very moving tribute to the young
Bernanos of this period has been paid by a young artisan friend
of these years, Henri Tilliette.[14]

His studies completed in 1913, Bernanos moved in October to
Rouen where he was named Editor-in-Chief of the local royalist
weekly newspaper *L'Avant-Garde de Normandie*. While holding
to the official *Action française* line of opposition to both Jews
and Freemasons, Bernanos nonetheless brought a certain element
of humanity to the hard doctrinaire line of the little paper. His
innate human compassion can be detected in his remarks about
French workers lined up against his side, seeing in them his
"brothers" who had been seduced by the claims of the enemy.[15]
In this paper Bernanos also fought against the philosopher Alain,
whose column was printed in the Rouen newspaper *La Dépêche*,
as well as against Lafond, the editor of another Rouen newspaper. In his own newspaper Bernanos was to publish three early
attempts at the short story. Although this brief venture as an
editor was a unique experience for Bernanos, it did serve to con-
firm in the future novelist his taste for creative writing as an
expression of a higher and more lasting vision than the ever-
changing scene of political interests.

V The War and the Founding of a Family: 1914–1919

When war broke out, Bernanos succeeded, in spite of his
deferment for reasons of health, to enlist once more in the Sixth
Regiment of Dragoons. He remained with his regiment through-

out the war, was wounded and was decorated, participating in the battles of Verdun and La Somme. Engaged to Jeanne Talbert d'Arc at the beginning of the war, he married this daughter of the president of the Royalist Ladies of Rouen and, it is claimed, a direct descendant of Joan of Arc's brother. The wedding took place at Vincennes on the eighteenth anniversary of Bernanos' first communion, May 11, 1917, in the middle of the war. The ceremony was performed by the noted royalist Benedictine, Dom Besse who, until his death in 1920, exercised a strong influence on the young man. Best man at the wedding was Maurras' assistant and one of the founders of *Action française*, the well-known novelist and literary critic Léon Daudet, son of Alphonse.

While Bernanos was recovering from injuries in 1917, his fiancée[16] had sent him the works of Léon Bloy. Bernanos was so profoundly moved by the Christian genius of this old master and his depiction of human injustice that he literally rolled in the grass in fury.[17] Since it is among Bloy's spiritual descendants, as much as among the literary descendants of Barbey d'Aurevilly, that Bernanos is seemingly best classified today, the violence accompanying this initial encounter is all the more significant.

On April 25th, 1918, a daughter was born to the young couple, the first of six children to be born in the years 1918–1933: Chantal, Yves, Claude, Michel, Dominique and Jean-Loup.

The war over, new responsibilities faced the young veteran, and employment had to be found. His father-in-law got him a job with his own employer, *La Nationale*, an insurance company. For seven years Bernanos was to work as an inspector, traveling in the eastern region of France, in that Lorraine of his own paternal ancestors.

Disgusted with the *Action française*'s decision to become a political party and send Léon Daudet as a deputy to the National Assembly, Bernanos, in the years immediately following the war, did not support the official "maurrasian" line; yet his sympathy for the cause remained unshaken. He was disgusted also by the empty victory of 1918, by the profiteering of the rich capitalists while the flower of French youth lay rotting on the battlefield.

The year 1919 also brought into Bernanos' life Robert Vallery-Radot, a minor Catholic poet and man of letters to whom Dom Besse introduced Bernanos at that same Institut Catholique where Bernanos had been a student.[18] The friendship that sprang up between Bernanos and Vallery-Radot was of singular importance for the aspiring young novelist since Vallery-Radot was editor of the Catholic review *L'Univers* and a prominent figure in the Catholic literary world in Paris. Besides his poetry, Vallery-Radot wrote a great number of books on many different subjects and was thus in a position to help launch his friend's work.

VI *The Struggle for Glory: 1920–1926*

It may be said that the friendship with Vallery-Radot was decisive for Bernanos. He no longer had the close contact he had once enjoyed with the great literary names of *Action française,* such as Léon Daudet; and his spiritual director, Dom Besse, himself well established in the world of letters, died in 1920, the year following his bringing together Bernanos and Vallery-Radot. Thus Vallery-Radot's role in gaining recognition for Bernanos is of great importance.

Vallery-Radot had one of Bernanos' short stories, "Madame Dargent," published by François Le Grix in the *Revue hebdomadaire* in 1922. Four years later he was responsible—alone responsible Bernanos avowed in a letter to his friend—for *Under the Sun of Satan*'s being published. The friendship of Vallery-Radot and his children can hardly be exaggerated in its importance. This is especially so of his daughter Marie who acted as a sort of young aunt for Bernanos' large family, taking various ones of the children to the Vallery-Radot country house in Avallon from time to time. Because Vallery-Radot was so faithful to the Bernanos family throughout numerous financial ups and downs, one can only view the two men as having been born for one another and Dom Besse's introduction as providential. A certain distance inevitably would come about as a result of all the tumultuous events of the Spanish Civil War, World War II and Bernanos' living outside of France from 1934 to 1937 and again from 1938 to 1945; yet Bernanos' devotion to the family of Vallery-Radot was evident at the end in his dedication of *The Carmelites* to Christiane Manificat, Marie Vallery-Radot's first cousin.

From 1919 to 1924 Bernanos and his family lived in Paris at 3,

rue de l'Université, taking advantage of the family home at
Fressin (not sold until 1925) for extended stays in the country
with the small children, of which there were four by 1924. Bernanos' work as an insurance inspector forced him to be away
from his family for extended periods in the eastern region of
France. During these years as an inspector Bernanos composed
his first novel. He worked on it as he traveled, weaving his
perennial solitude as well as his disgust of the post-war world
into the story of a priest-saint's frightening struggle with Satan
in whom Bernanos, true to his Christian formation, saw the true
enemy of the race and the seducer of all mankind.

Bernanos is believed to have begun work on this novel in
1919.[19] In the spring and early summer of 1923 he underwent
a terrible illness involving an abscess and a perforated intestine.
This grave illness would appear to have had some effect upon
his feelings about the novel since, he later stated, he thought he
was going to die but did not want to die without having "wit-
nessed." His intention in writing this, as well as the rest of his
novels—not to speak of the polemical work—may be said to be,
therefore, of a prophetic character, prophetic in the sense of the
Old Testament prophets, the *nabîm*, who bore witness to the
truth of affairs rather than foretold future disasters. However, in
Bernanos, as in a Baudelaire or a Rimbaud, both elements are
to be found; they are particularly evident in a novel such as
M. Ouine.

The year 1923 also brought to the fore another factor which
was to shape Bernanos' personal life: Madame Bernanos' health.
The beginning of tuberculosis was diagnosed at the same time
Bernanos was suffering his own terrible illness of abscess and
pierced intestine. A trip to Lourdes in that summer seemed to
have helped his wife, but in 1926 a lethargic encephalitis was
diagnosed. In the years which followed, her physical strength
was hardly of that energetic robustness necessary to face crushing
poverty and the responsibility for a family of six children. The
account of the illnesses of the children and of Bernanos' inability
to feed them in those lean years of 1930 to 1937 still strikes horror
in the mind of his most sympathetic reader. One finds admirable
the fact that Bernanos himself survived until he was sixty, his
wife surviving him by twelve years. The Bernanos family situa-

tion will, no doubt, some day be compared to the better known case of the household of Léon Bloy where Lady Poverty was also a too frequent guest.

At the beginning of the year 1925, Bernanos installed his family at Bar-le-Duc in Lorraine, a more central location for him in his travels in eastern France. In February, just after getting installed on "an old street of an old city in a house of the same age," Bernanos announced to Vallery-Radot that he had completed his book.[20] Since Léon Daudet did not read the manuscript which Bernanos had hopefully sent him, Vallery-Radot alone was responsible for seeing that the work appeared.

Vallery-Radot presented the manuscript to Plon. Henri Massis liked the work and decided to publish it in Plon's Roseau d'Or series which he, Jacques Maritain and Frédéric Lefèvre directed, with Stanislas Fumet as secretary. Friendship between Massis and Bernanos sprang up at this point. The very warm tone of Bernanos' letters to the author of *Maurras et son temps* reveals that depth of faith and affection with which Bernanos so generously surrounded all those for whom he felt a profound sympathy.

VII *Glory: 1926–1929*

With the publication of *Under the Sun of Satan* in March, 1926, Bernanos was immediately catapulted to literary glory. Sales far exceeded expectations, and demands for translations soon brought international fame. As a result of this quite unexpected good fortune, Bernanos made one of the most momentous decisions of his life from a practical point of view: he would henceforth give himself to writing alone, depending upon his pen for supporting his family.

This decision has often since been commented on by those who saw at firsthand what the writer and his family were to suffer from the lack of a sure, fixed income. One former friend[21] said he even suggested to Bernanos that his insurance company would probably give him a good job in Paris, since they would be honored with having a famous writer as one of their employees —a possibility quite in keeping with the usual esteem accorded writers in France, even by insurance companies. Indeed, Bernanos had been given a company promotion and pay increase in 1925, and a further reward for heaping honor on *La Nationale* would undoubtedly have been forthcoming.

Yet within the author himself there was a thirst for glory and a feeling for the absolute which forbade all compromise. As a youth, he had asked God for two things: the necessities of life and glory. Glory was now his and, he undoubtedly felt, would remain his if it were possible for him to turn out, at a bit more rapid pace, the revelation of his interior world with which he had filled his first novel. As for the necessities, Bernanos was to remark towards the end of his life that God had, of course, answered this part of his prayer too, except that he himself would never have believed that the necessities could be reduced to such a minimum.[22]

With his thirst for glory, Bernanos also must have chafed under the burdensome necessities of his work as an agent for an insurance company. The irony which his later life was to provide—where he shows us a life insured against nothing, not even against lack of food—would serve to convince one that the writer was too much of a poet ever to believe in the prudent policies of *La Nationale* or of any other insurance company. There must thus have been a considerable sense of release and relief as the thirty-eight-year-old author resigned from the only job he ever held for any period of time.

A man with less integrity than Bernanos, a man with less deep spiritual involvement with everything he wrote, could, of course, have lived by his pen. Bernanos had received a unique and powerful launching as a writer with his first novel. Léon Daudet's enthusiastic statement in the *Action française*[23] that here at last was the true post-war writer, here now was the writer in whom he saw greatness comparable to that of Proust (whose work he had also hailed), was destined to attract favor to the new and unknown writer.

And, indeed, Bernanos did make an effort to become a proper man of letters. Moving to the south of France in the summer of 1926, in view of recommendations concerning Madame Bernanos' health, the family settled for almost a year near Lourdes at Bagnières-de-Bigorre. There Bernanos worked at the novel destined to become *L'Imposture*. However, condemnation in the autumn of that year of the *Action française* by Pope Pius XI provoked in him an immediate sympathy for his condemned friends and former associates as well as bitter reaction to the scandal of depriving Catholic youth of the sacraments because they saw in the *Action française* a means to restore France's past—and Christian—heritage.

"Saint Dominique," a short article on that saint, and a work typical of what a really aspiring Catholic man of letters should turn out in quantity every year, was published in November in *La Revue Universelle.* Two months later, in January, 1927, Bernanos' father died of the same illness which, twenty-one years later, would kill Bernanos: disease of the liver. Prophetically enough, Bernanos wrote Vallery-Radot as his father lay dying: "I am experiencing my own death agony."[24]

In that same month of January, 1927, Bernanos refused the *Légion d'Honneur,* a refusal he was to repeat twice again, in 1938 and in 1946, demonstrating thereby his proud independence from all official honors.

L'Imposture was finished in March, and that summer Bernanos visited La Salette, the scene of the apparition of the Mother of God in the mid-nineteenth century and a place of pilgrimage made famous by Léon Bloy and his illustrious convert Jacques Maritain. While in that southern part of France, he also visited Ars, the life of whose famous curé saint had so inspired Bernanos as he wrote *Under the Sun of Satan.* Then, sure of the brightness of the future, Bernanos bought a large house at Clermont-de-l'Oise where the family was to have three relatively peaceful years before the onslaught of the thirties.

In November, 1927, *L'Imposture* appeared, and Bernanos received a moving letter from the poet Antonin Arthaud praising him for the scene of Abbé Chevance's death.[25] The book, however, was not a general success, and already Bernanos was at work on its sequel. The year 1928 also saw the beginning of another literary project: the "biography" of that master of Bernanos' youth, Edouard Drumont. This project, begun in the summer of 1928, would, for the moment, yield to Bernanos' more primary obligation of completing *Joy,* sequel to *L'Imposture. Joy* was finished in December of 1928, a year in which Bernanos had once more taken part in *Action française* rallies, using his new-found fame to support Maurras and followers such as Massis. A fifth child, his daughter Dominique, was also born this year.

Joy was published in April, 1929, and, in December, Bernanos received the *Prix Fémina,* underlining for the writer the good chance he had for success as a man of letters. He published during this same year his little essay on Joan of Arc, *Jeanne relapse et sainte,* underlining how the official Church had legally condemned her and yet how God had avenged her. This idea has been brought out in the title given the English translation of this short work *Sanctity Will Out.* One can sense, perhaps, an attempt at a subtle reply to the papal condemnation of the *Action française* in this work, since Bernanos takes the trouble to point out that the papal legate's signature figured in her condemnation and that her appeal to the pope was completely meaningless and out of order, since the papal representative was personally present already. The *Revue hebdomadaire,* which had published Bernanos' first major short story "'Madame Dargent" in 1922, also published this hagiographical essay.

VIII   *Failure: 1930–1935*

Since his third novel had won a literary prize in December, 1929, and since his family was established in the large house he had purchased at Clermont-de-l'Oise, Bernanos must have looked forward to 1930 with some confidence. However, his mother's illness, diagnosed in the fall of 1929 as a fatal tuberculosis of the kidneys, led to her death in March, 1930. This was not destined to soothe the writer's tranquility, already disturbed by the composition of the tempestuous book on Drumont which he was pushing to completion. Jean de Fabrègues states that the absence of Massis at Bernanos' mother's funeral was the first indication Bernanos had of a rupture in their friendship.[26] Regardless of the factors which brought about this rupture, Bernanos' letters to Massis since the beginning of their friendship in 1925 show, as has been previously mentioned, an extremely warm affection on Bernanos' part. This rupture with a close friend was no doubt the sign of a great turmoil within the writer at this period, and it is not surprising that he went to Vesenex in the

département of Ain in the summer of 1930 to receive treatment
for a nervous disorder. Prolonging his stay, Bernanos completed
La Grande peur des bien-pensants and spent the entire summer
there before going on with his family to install themselves at
Toulon on France's southern coast.

In April, 1931, *La Grande peur des bien-pensants* appeared. But
already Bernanos had returned to his writing of novels. *Night Is
Darkest* was begun at the start of the new year, only to be interrupted in February when he initiated another novel, the great,
ill-fated masterpiece *M. Ouine.* Bernanos had begun this novel,
he wrote Vallery-Radot, "because the first one disgusted me."[27]
This year, too, marks the beginning of a certain financial pressure
from which Bernanos and his family would suffer over the next
six years. Bernanos' name was established, and a new review,
Réaction, edited by a young admirer of Bernanos, Jean de Fabrègues, even dedicated a whole issue to him. Moreover, Vallery-
Radot, who had become literary editor of *Le Figaro,* now the
property of the wealthy perfume manufacturer, François Coty,
used his influence to obtain work for Bernanos as a writer of
articles for the paper. In November this journalistic collaboration
began. Yet, in December, Bernanos was already uneasy about the
reception his articles would arouse in his new patron, and, as he
avowed to Vallery-Radot, he had good reason to worry since
"if this collaboration were withdrawn from me in a month, I
literally don't know how I'd live."

Bernanos' fears did not subside with the advent of a new year.
On January 12 he wrote Vallery-Radot that Coty had indeed
settled up with him for the articles he had contributed to date,
but that the accompanying letter was neither reassuring nor unfavorable. In the same letter Bernanos asked Vallery-Radot to
discover discreetly how the future with *Le Figaro* stood, since
all of this was quite literally a question of his daily bread.

But the worst was yet to come. *Action française,* which regarded *Le Figaro* an enemy, launched an attack on Coty in
regard to a political manoeuvre. Bernanos, feeling he himself was
also being aimed at, wrote a defense of his new patron, thereby
launching a violent, passionate polemic between Maurras and
Bernanos. None of the past was held sacred, and all dirty linen,
real or imagined, was exposed to the public. In a dramatic high-

flung letter which appeared, of course, in print, Maurras, the master of Bernanos' youthful passion, wrote: "Bernanos, I say Adieu to you." Bernanos replied with another letter in print with his own "Adieu, Maurras! I leave you to God's sweet mercy." Bernanos, one can imagine, regretted the useless deployment of his energies and the useless enmity which this polemic served to establish between himself and those who were to remain faithful to Maurras. Bernanos' final "Adieu" appeared in May, 1932, and, on June 24, Bernanos announced his departure from *Le Figaro*. His articles, however, would continue to appear until December.[28]

Returning to the writing of *M. Ouine*, Bernanos, in December, 1932, was well into that novel. He came to regard it as his greatest, and the year 1933 might thus well have proved to be the year in which he would achieve new fame and replenish his dwindling account at his publishers. Indeed, in April, 1933, Bernanos foresaw completing his "great novel" by the end of the year,[29] little suspecting that the loss of three scenes which had disappeared during one of his motorcycle trips that month would interrupt the flow of his work.

Two of these three lost scenes, all of which come at a crucial point in the book's evolution, would never be rewritten.[30] This is all the more significant when one remembers that just prior to this, while Bernanos must have been submerged in writing these sections of *M. Ouine*, he had written Vallery-Radot: "I've never been so happy" and then "My only fear is you won't like my book."[31]

In May, 1933, the family moved to a large house at La Bayorre, still in the general vicinity of Toulon, and Bernanos' financial situation became an increasing source of anxiety. Worse was yet to come. Madame Bernanos expected their sixth child in September. Two months before the expected birth, Bernanos went off on his motorcycle to Avallon with all the manuscript pages of *M. Ouine* that he had finished up to that time—about two thirds of the novel. In Avallon he read it to Vallery-Radot who was trying to assist him financially by arranging for an advance luxury edition of the coming work. Coming back by way of Montbéliard, Bernanos was struck by a car. The author's leg was crushed, and the expenses of hospitalization plus the physical suffering which forbade any thought of work proved the source of much anguish to the author.

Jean-Loup, the sixth and last child, arrived in September at a moment when Bernanos was ready to show Vallery-Radot some two hundred or more pages of his novel. By November, suffering from neuritis, Bernanos was becoming anxious about reaching some accord with Plon so that he and his family could at least survive. He was thus led to propose to Vallery-Radot that his friend see if Plon would argee to pay him by the page. In that way he could draw on his royalties in advance and thus utilize, to a more immediate advantage, work that he had in progress. Such an arrangement would, as we shall see, eventually be worked out the following year, and the author's most famous novel, *Diary of a Country Priest,* would actually be sent in packets of twenty or thirty pages to Paris so that money needed to buy bread would be forthcoming by return mail.

Feeling that *M. Ouine* was his most immediate concern, Bernanos assembled the first thirteen of the novel's eventual nineteen chapters, copied them out and sent them to Paris in the spring of 1934. In August of this year he undertook the writing of a detective story which his publishers thought an excellent way for him to straighten out his accounts. But even a detective story is not written and published in a month's time, and Bernanos' landlord was becoming impatient for the sum due him for the large villa the family had taken at La Bayorre. At this point Bernanos' suggestion that Plon advance him royalties for every finished page he sent in was made into an official agreement.

Yet the situation, even with the new agreement with Plon, proved irreparable. Abandoning the family belongings, his books and papers, which the landlord disposed of to recompense himself as best he could for the unpaid rent, Bernanos departed in October with his large family for the Spanish island of Majorca. There they hoped to be able to live more easily on the small sum which Bernanos would, it was assumed, glean from Plon as he turned in his pages.

Later, recalling this period, Bernanos said it had been a veritable nightmare to hear his wife and children crying at him each morning: "Your pages, Papa! Your pages."[32] Yet, in December, 1934, after supposedly finishing his detective novel and while working on *M. Ouine,* Bernanos began what was to prove his most famous book: *Diary of a Country Priest.*

However, the conclusion of the detective novel was not acceptable to Plon, and so Bernanos was forced from February to May, 1935, to rewrite the ending of *A Crime.* In this second writing, the ending became two parts—a second and a third part instead of just a single second part. On completion of this, Bernanos worked from June to August on the returned pages of the original second part (for which he had already been paid)and incorporated them into *Night Is Darkest.*[33] Thus, by August, 1935, he had also completed *Night Is Darkest. A Crime,* however, had appeared just the month before and was not very well received.

It is impossible to say whether it was the author's fear of another critical defeat or merely that he preferred to get back to *Diary of a Country Priest* that made him defer sending off a fair copy of *Night Is Darkest* to Paris. Perhaps the income from *A Crime,* slight though it was, helped relieve the financial pressure. In any case, in September, 1935, Bernanos returned to the writing of *Diary of a Country Priest* and finished it at the end of January 1936.

IX *New Departure: 1936–1939*

In March, 1936, *Diary of a Country Priest* was published in Paris, its success surpassing even that of ten years earlier when *Under the Sun of Satan* was published. Critics, readers and the French Academy were all in accord that this was a great novel, and the latter group even accorded its *Grand Prix du Roman* to Bernanos for the work. Now full of confidence, Bernanos took up once more his "great novel" *M. Ouine.* In fact, he actually completed all but the final chapter (XIX) of the novel in which he was to describe the last agony to the old professor-hero. Although both the seventeenth and eighteenth chapters, written during this period, are situated at M. Ouine's deathbed, Bernanos seems to have found it impossible to bring about the old man's death.[34] Moreover, just after he had sent off these chapters in July, 1936, the Spanish Civil War reached the shores of Majorca, imported from the mainland.

In *A Diary of My Times,* the book Bernanos would eventually write on what he saw take place in Majorca, he tells how the

Civil War arrived on the island and how the peasants were loaded on trucks and taken off and shot. In this reign of terror Bernanos saw a prefiguration of what was to come as a logical result of modern bourgeois democratic "order." Although his sixteen-year-old son Yves was a lieutenant on Franco's side, fighting with the *Falange*, Bernanos saw that there was no human compassion on either side, that each side answered fear with its own fear. For him this crisis in the modern world was provoked by the disintegration of Christianity and because man had lost the taste even for that joy and freedom in God which Christianity gave man. The Christian implications of this crisis were especially underlined in Bernanos' reflections on war and through his magnificent "sermon of the non-believer" to a congregation of Christians.

Besides *A Diary of My Times*, this conflict was also to be responsible for Bernanos' last novel, *Mouchette*. He undertook this work in the second half of 1936 as reaction to seeing innocent, uncomprehending people shot for just what reason no one was quite sure.[35] *Mouchette* was published in May, 1937. Though such a short novel (it has even been termed a long short story), it is a stylistic *tour de force* in which Bernanos excelled himself as a master describing the suffering of an adolescent.

In March, 1937, two months before *Mouchette* was published, Bernanos and his family left Majorca and returned to the south of France. There, because he had lost his first manuscript of his book on the Spanish Civil War—fragments of which had been published in the Dominican review *Sept* between June, 1936, and January, 1937—Bernanos was obliged to write a new version of this highly controversial book. Bernanos worked at *A Diary of My Times* from May, 1937, following the publication of *Mouchette*, until April, 1938. This work, Bernanos said, would be published even if he had to pay for it himself. He felt that some Catholic had to speak up about the abuses the hierarchy of the Church in Majorca were allowing, whereby a person who did not have a ticket saying he had received the sacraments at Easter could be shot as a Communist.

The stir caused by the publication of *A Diary of My Times* was violent. The reactions of its readers were roughly the same as those which, three years later, were to be their reactions to the more general conflict. Regardless of which camp the reader chose, it was not likely that he would be led to alter his allegiance even when the horrors of Nazi Germany became involved. *Action française* felt Bernanos had definitely gone over to the hated enemy; the Jesuits condemned the book, and there were even threats that it would be put on the Index by the Vatican. Bernanos' widow reported in 1957 that Pope Pius XI had been encouraged to read the book before condemning it. After a night spent devouring it, the pontiff stated that the Vatican would never condemn Bernanos since he had written the truth.[36]

It is also highly significant that Simone Weil, who herself had taken the train for Spain to fight on the Communist side, had been burned in an accident and brought back to Paris by her parents, also found that Bernanos had told nothing but the truth in this volume. In a long and very beautiful letter addressed to Bernanos,[37] she expresses her appreciation of his witness and says that the truth brings them together despite the fact that Bernanos had an anti-Semitic master and a son who had fought on the opposite side in the Spanish conflict.

After *A Diary of My Times* appeared in May, 1938, Bernanos had, for the first time in several years, been able to amass a bit of money. The conflict about to break in Europe may well have been partly responsible for his decision now to leave France once more. He had also longed, ever since his youthful days as a student, to join the old student comrades of his "Men of War" group who had taken the boat for Paraguay. In any case, just two months before the Munich Pact in July, 1938, Bernanos and his family took the boat for South America.

His hope of realizing his old dream of living in Paraguay was not possible with his large family, however, and he left that country for Brazil after less than two weeks. Thus Brazil was to become his home for almost seven years, from September, 1938, until July, 1945.

Here, in Brazil, Bernanos devoted himself exclusively to nonfiction, with the exception of the last chapter of *M. Ouine* which he would complete in the first half of 1940. In January, 1939, Bernanos finished *Scandale de la vérité*, giving his reaction to the Munich Pact and his feelings regarding Maurras. After this came *Nous autres Français* finished in June.

X *France Alone: 1940–1945*

From September, 1939, until June, 1940, Bernanos optimistically set himself up as the head of a great estate for the exploitation of cattle, the *fazenda San Antonio* near Pirapora. This short-lived attempt was, needless to say, disastrous. However, in Pirapora the author had completed *Les Enfants humiliés* by January, and then, from February to May, 1940, he wrote the last great chapter of *M. Ouine.*

With the armistice, Bernanos felt immediate revulsion, and in reply to the appeal of June 18, 1940, his two elder sons, Yves and Michel, as well as Guy Hattu, the nephew who had accompanied the family to Brazil, answered General de Gaulle's challenge. Bernanos himself undertook the task of sustaining the Free French with his pen since his lameness forbade active duty.

In August, 1940, he bought what was to remain his home for the next four years, a small farm near Barbecena at Cruz des Almas—"The Cross of Souls"—so named because it was the site where Christians had been martyred. Here he waited the war out, writing his reaction to the daily news bulletins in articles which were published between 1942 and 1944 in collections under the name of *Le Chemin de la Croix-des-Ames.*[38]

For Brazilian newspapers in Rio de Janeiro, for *La Marseillaise* of London and Algiers, and for the *Bulletins* of Free France, Bernanos supplied articles filled with his own unique and persuasive fervor. When the *Dublin Review* requested a long article from him in 1941, he turned out his unusual volume, *Plea for Liberty (Lettre aux Anglais),* published in Rio de Janeiro in 1942. *Tradition of Freedom (La France contre les robots)* in 1944 betrayed an anxiety Bernanos shared with that other great spirit of his day, Simone Weil, as they faced the problem of man who becomes the servant of the inhuman demands of the machine.

Bernanos' articles and books were secretly printed and circulated in Europe, earning for him the title of "The Animator of the Resistance." The love and hope he inspired in many of the youths of the French Resistance appears, unfortunately, to have led to more being expected of him than he—or any mortal being—could possibly give once the war was over.[39] The fact is that Bernanos' great genius was that of seeing and stating the precise nature of the problem, not in providing an answer to it or a way out of it.

Perhaps in the hope that Bernanos might be able to supply an answer, General de Gaulle sent for him three different times in Brazil, appealing with a telegram which read, "Your place is here among us." From Bernanos' Benedictine friend of the time, Dom Paul Gordon, it would appear that Bernanos himself was not so sure where his place was at that time. Dom Paul reports that a severe nervous crisis resulted over Bernanos' indecision about what was best to do, and it was only with some reluctance and on the Benedictine's counsel that he finally decided to return to that France he loved too much to admit her imperfections. It even seems doubtful that his decision would have been reached had the Benedictine not told him that he should go back to his country. This he did in July, 1945, regarding his return, it would seem, as an act of spiritual obedience.

XI *The Return: 1945-1948*

Exactly three years were left the author now, and they were not to be tranquil ones. Collaborating with numerous Parisian newspapers *(La Bataille, Combat, Carrefour, Le Figaro, L'Intransigeant)*, Bernanos was also called upon for public appearances and lectures at the Sorbonne, in Geneva and in Belgium where he continued to warn against the dangers to man's freedom and the threat of totalitarian thought.

Offered a portfolio in de Gaulle's provisional government as Minister of Education,[40] Bernanos refused, just as he also refused at this time to solicit a seat in the French Academy[41] when well-placed friends urged him to do so from their conviction that his candidature would be successful. Bernanos jokingly remarked that, though he had been offered a seat in the Academy and a Minister's Portfolio, he had not yet been offered the place of an archbishop. Undoubtedly there was actually only one glory which Bernanos would have prized above all others, and that was the place of a saint. He even once expressed his regret at not having become a saint so that he could provide the imbeciles with a patron!

A certain tragic, even bitter, note is evident throughout this last period when Bernanos believed that no one understood his vision of what threatened man. Constantly tormented by the thought that France had been humiliated by the armistice and that Pétain's government was the height of dishonor since it had abandoned France's allies, Bernanos continued to articulate his anguish in newspaper articles. We are told even that he still threatened to leave France, return to South America and renounce his nationality in order to cause his admirers to reflect that France had fallen very low indeed if Bernanos refused to be called French.[42]

In 1947 he left France for North Africa, settling in Tunisia, first in Hammamet, then in Gabbès. One of Bernanos' most important last statements was made during this North African stay when he addressed a group of nuns belonging to Père de Foucauld's order. In this address he elucidates his views of the ties between sanctity and freedom.[43]

It was in Tunisia, during his last earthly winter of 1947–1948, that, Bernanos, undoubtedly aware that he himself was reaching the end, wrote the work that was to be his spiritual testament, *The Carmelites*. This work, conceived and written as the simple dialogues for a film scenario which Bernanos' Dominican friend, Father Bruckberger, and film producer, Philippe Agostini, had written (based on the story *Die Letzte am Schaffot* by Gertrude von le Fort), became a little masterpiece destined for the theater as well as the operatic stage when Francis Poulenc would set it to music. In *The Carmelites* Bernanos treated two ideas which were especially near to him at the moment: fear of death and French honor. Completed in mid-March just as Bernanos was obliged to take to his bed for the last time, this work was revealed only after the author's death.

When his wealthy friend Henri Jacques, with whom he had become linked in Brazil, heard of Bernanos' condition, he had him flown back to Paris to the American Hospital. There he was to succumb on July 5, 1948. The description of the last six weeks of Bernanos' life, as revealed in the beautiful account left by the young priest who attended him, Abbé Daniel Pezeril, reveals that until the very end Bernanos continued to wage the spiritual battle, amassing his forces for God against the enemy of the race. When the priest told Bernanos before his operation that his work

would intercede to God for him, he replied, "I am not responsible
for what I have written. I am responsible for what I have not
been."[44]

Thus it was that on the June, 30, 1948, five days before he
entered into his last agony, Bernanos confided to the priest that
he had renounced not only writing novels but also even writing
for France. Henceforth only God would occupy his energies:
he would, if God restored him to health, consecrate himself to
the *Life of Jesus,* a work which he had projected for some time.
To Abbé Pezeril in whom Bernanos confided this decision as
"having said 'Yes' to God," this act was his final movement of
acceptance before leaving this life. In an even larger perspective
it is possible to see in this act an attempt on Bernanos' part to
imitate his beloved St. Thérèse of Lisieux who told God she had
nothing to offer Him but Himself and, therefore, that He must
clothe her to appear before Him. In offering to God nothing but
a *Life of Jesus,* the author, like Thérèse, offered to the Creator
nothing which was not Himself.[45]

One incident, reported by Abbé Pezeril as happening on the
Saturday preceding Bernanos' death on Monday morning, casts
a rare light on the man behind the author. After Bernanos' daily
reception of Holy Communion, the priest always prayed with
him. While they prayed the Lord's Prayer that morning, Madame
Bernanos and two of their daughters entered the room. Bernanos
was seated, his hands joined and held high. When the priest
articulated the words "but deliver us from evil," Bernanos cried
out with a loud voice, "Yes, Father! Father, through your son
Jesus Christ, don't hurt me any more." He repeated this again
and again, shattering the composure of priest and family, until
Abbé Pezeril finally persuaded him to lie down again. Then the
dying author turned to the priest and asked, "Do you believe
that the dear Lord will forgive me my sins?"[46]

At about four o'clock on his last afternoon, as he realized that
the end was upon him, Bernanos remarked to his wife, "Now
I'm caught in the Holy Agony," thereby again attesting, and for
the last time, the importance which the mystery of Christ's agony
in the garden played in his own interior life. Abbé Pezeril arrived
at six o'clock. The last vigil had begun.

Bernanos now called for his mother. The attending nurse, undoubtedly thinking she had a simple case of a wandering mind to deal with, said, "Wait a minute and I'll go get her out in the hall." One can imagine her surprise when Bernanos, completely lucid, answered, "Oh no you won't, since she's dead." Thus invoking his dead mother, Bernanos advanced towards the last portals of mortality. Rousing just before midnight, he uttered that defiant cry he had probably first encountered as a youth reading Balzac: "A nous deux" ("It's up to us two"). Defiance of death, of Satan, or a final struggle for God? One can only speculate.

At five o'clock in the morning, breathing his wife's name while she prayed the Lord's Prayer and the Hail Mary, Bernanos, lucid to the end, expired. The peace which was evident on his face and which can still be seen in photographs of him on his deathbed is striking. His tormented spirit had found rest and peace at the last.

In January, before leaving North Africa, Bernanos had written in his agenda lines which elucidate, no doubt, the source of that extraordinary peace remarked upon by those who viewed him on his deathbed. These lines, written as he worked at *The Carmelites*, are a commentary on the spiritual depth of this author. Written on the pages of the agenda for the 24th and 25th of January,[47] below routine notes revealing that it was windy, that Bernanos had, on the 24th, a Saturday, been to visit the Blessed Sacrament and on Sunday, the 25th, had been to "Holy Mass," we find these lines:

We really want what He wants. We really want our pains, our suffering and solitude without being aware of it since we imagine we only want our pleasures. We think we dread and flee our death when we really want it, just as He wanted His—besides, our death is His death. In the same way that He offers Himself in sacrifice on every altar where the Mass is celebrated, so also He again dies once more in every dying man. We want everything that He wants but we do not know ourselves—sin makes us live on the surface of our beings; we only go back into ourselves to die, and it is there that He awaits us.

Part II

The Work

CHAPTER 1

Images, Patterns and Themes

THE theme of childhood dominates Bernanos' fiction.[1] The most common manifestation of this theme is seen in the recurrent pattern of a suffering adolescent crushed by circumstances beyond his comprehension. Two other images of childhood are also frequently evoked throughout the author's work: first, that of childhood innocence which, as it were, rises up as a protective force in the hour of need in adult life; secondly, the beautiful, evangelical image of becoming a child again, especially, in Bernanos, as one confronts death.

The primacy of childhood as theme will, of course, be challenged by a good majority of those critics who have mistaken the frequently encountered image of the priest for Bernanos' major theme.[2] While it is certainly true that Bernanos, armed with an unusually powerful and penetrating psychological insight which permitted him to probe the depths of the interior life of all his major characters, has spared no aspect of the inner life of the priest, and while good priests and bad priests alike, both equally convincing in their struggles, come to life for the reader, yet to regard the character of the priest as the central theme necessarily excludes half of Bernanos' fiction. Thus, although his best known and perhaps his most successful novel is, and will remain, *Diary of a Country Priest*, and although both his second and third novels, *L'Imposture* and *Joy* respectively, turn around the drama of the redemption of a single non-believing priest, yet the priest is absent from *Mouchette* and is of only secondary importance in *M. Ouine, Night Is Darkest* and, in a sense, in *A Crime*. Moreover, even in his first novel, *Under the Sun of Satan*, which usually rather shocks the reader as he encounters the temptations of the priest-saint in his battles with Satan both within and without himself, Bernanos had already felt the need to balance his priest

53

by the presence of a "humiliated child," a crushed, disappointed adolescent.

Even when the author attempted to deal with other themes, the mystery of childhood kept intruding. In both *Night Is Darkest* and, to a certain extent, in *M. Ouine*, Bernanos dealt with the washed-out, used-up generation which survived World War I. Yet, even so, in both of these books the author envisaged what each of the major characters had suffered in his youth, what humiliations had been overcome and how this victory is continually paid for in adult life. The same phenomenon can be observed in Bernanos' one detective novel, *A Crime*, a book he wrote only for money and in which he took no pride. In this strange story the murderess kills both an old woman and the priest, a new arrival in the village who has not yet been seen by anyone. The murderess strips the young man, dons his cassock, and masquerades as the new priest while the old woman's killer is being sought. Thus, although the priest as an image is present, it is truly neither a novel about a priest nor, for that matter, about a man; rather, it is about a criminal woman whose greatest grace is her unhappy childhood, a childhood which can even be said to be cursed since she herself is the child of a defrocked nun and, quite probably, a priest. Finally, *Mouchette*, Bernanos' last conceived novel—only the last great chapter of *M. Ouine* would be written after it—deals only with the theme of humiliated adolescence: the young heroine is raped and finally commits suicide.

Death by suicide is, indeed, another common pattern for Bernanos' adolescents. Yet, strangely enough, their suicides are always born of their honor which, rather than surrender, they prefer to risk in a last supreme effort of taking their own life. The first Mouchette in *Under the Sun of Satan* cuts her throat, then asks to be carried to the church to die. In *A Crime*, the altar boy; in *Night Is Darkest*, Philippe; in *Mouchette*, the heroine; all these adolescents seek death after a shattering disappointment. For Bernanos honored risk and believed it to be the great characteristic of heroes, saints and martyrs as well as a virtue especially belonging to youth. His "children" thus consistently answered the disappointment which assaulted them by risking everything in one last gesture.

Characters other than Bernanos' adolescents, however, also

resort to suicide: the non-believing priest, Abbé Cénabre, goes through the motion of shooting himself while his former penitent, Pernichon, actually succeeds in an attempt at taking his own life. The drug-addicted Russian chauffeur in *Joy* kills himself after slaughtering the novel's heroine, Chantal de Clergerie; both the murderess in *A Crime* and her defrocked-nun mother kill themselves; the lovers in *M. Ouine* die in a double suicide; finally, the non-believing doctor in *Diary of a Country Priest* shoots himself.[3] If one objects that so much suicide seems rather excessive, it must be recalled that, in trying to portray the deeper truths of the mystery of human life, Bernanos became aware of the preoccupation of contemporary man whose civilization continues to plunge him towards a mass suicide.

Yet there is also an aesthetic aspect in Bernanos' choice of the adolescent as his central figure since such a youth is an excellent image of man as he encounters the truth of life and death. Indeed, the disappointments of adolescence seem to become only more intense in later life as they change form and gradually bring man, still suffering from hopes unfulfilled, to death. Thus, although Bernanos' rational search for a perfect hero seemed to have drawn him towards the priest, his intuitive sense insisted on a more universal—if less exalted—image: the suffering adolescent.[4]

Perhaps it is Bernanos' preoccupation with the human aspects of man that caused him to choose these ever-recurring images and patterns. He condemned German heroism—that of a superman such as Siegfried—and contrasted it with French heroism—that of Roland, the epic hero who dies defeated, but in a manner becoming to his humanity as God's vassal. Bernanos' orientation towards the human limitations of man are to be seen also as part of his extraordinarily deep penetration of the mysteries of Christianity. At a moment when conversions to Catholicism were very much in fashion, Bernanos jokingly remarked on his publisher's biographical form that he was a Catholic but did not have the honor of being a convert, intimating thereby what he always was to maintain: the Church was home to him, and he expressed himself in the Church as would a member of any large family. Indeed, the image of the family is also part of his very human approach not only to existence itself, but also to his patriotism and to his whole experience of God.

The experience of God is perhaps the most strikingly unusual theme of Bernanos' work. If one may say that *any* experience of God is mysticism, then one must surely say that there is a very great mystical side to Bernanos. Not that his mysticism soared off to ethereal heights; on the contrary, it was the most down-to-earth, day-by-day application of what was, for Bernanos, absolute truth: God had become man. With his very keen historical sense Bernanos realized that France's history, from Clovis to Louis XVI, was a result of his countrymen's application of this belief to their daily lives, to their institutions, to their way of thinking, acting, speaking and writing.

Referring to Bernanos' religion, many have tried to summarize it by saying that it is a religion of the "Beatitudes," and surely a certain truth is in that statement. Bernanos himself disclaimed all knowledge of formal theology other than what he had learned at his mother's knee: his catechism. But neither the catechism nor the Beatitudes answer completely the question raised when a noted German-Swiss theologian, Hans Urs von Balthazar, dedicates a large volume to Bernanos,[5] discussing the theological implications of his work in great detail. Nor do the Beatitudes and the catechism explain the surprise that nuns and priests experience as they find that this layman and father of six children had an intimate insight into their own spiritual struggles and temptations. What, then, more than the Beatitudes and the catechism is there behind Bernanos' Christianity?

The answer to this question bears, of course, on what Bernanos was and on what God was for him. One has only to read his youthful letters written to Abbé Lagrange, his former professor, to realize that Bernanos' interior life—that life of prayer and promises to God, that life of constant reference to, and communication with, the Absolute—was already, at the age of sixteen, highly developed. And it was in the depths of this highly developed interior life that were to be conceived all of Bernanos' major characters, whether saints or sinners. The fusion in Bernanos of both height and depth as one looks at man would seem to lie behind the comparison of his work with that of Dostoyevsky who, like Bernanos, was not content to show merely the depths of man's degradation, but also the spiritual heights to which he could soar.

Surely from Bernanos' interior life came his preoccupation with the agony of Christ in the Garden of Gethsemane, an image given considerable scope in *Joy* and *The Carmelites*. Both Péguy, much admired by Bernanos, and Pascal can be said to have treated this same image before him in an equally probing manner and in contrast to de Vigny's unchristian treatment. As he was entering his last hours on the night of July 4, 1948, Bernanos observed, "Now I am caught in the Holy Agony." This was the statement upon whose significance he had so amply meditated in *The Carmelites*, the work he had completed the very day he became definitively bed-ridden a few months before his death.

The path leading from suffering innocence to the agony in the garden is, therefore, the one the reader must take in encountering Bernanos' work. To a great extent it is, of course, still an image of the suffering innocence one encounters in the Garden of Gethsemane, and there can be no doubt that Bernanos sought to raise the implications of the suffering innocent to the cosmic heights of expiatory suffering of which the crucifixion of Christ is, for the Christian, the supreme image.

One can even note a certain evolution in Bernanos' work around this Christian theme of expiation.[6] His first three novels, *Under the Sun of Satan*, *L'Imposture* and *Joy* all show saints suffering for sinners, a classic Catholic concept dear to Claudel. Bernanos, however, abandoned it in his last five novels, leaving in them the resolution of "who suffers for whom" in the hands of God alone. Trusting more and more in the mystery of "God's sweet mercy," as he liked to put it, Bernanos thus moves towards a more definitive exaltation of the *mystery* of God's workings rather than towards a definition of the mystery.

The realization that the suffering of the innocent is not only an image of the human condition but also of the agony of Christ in Gethsemane is bound eventually to raise the question of the relationship between man's personal attitude towards himself and that of his role in the garden of suffering innocents. Bernanos learned at some point that hatred of self is the most dangerous of temptations, the one that leads straight into despair. In his first novel this temptation pushes the priest-hero to a ferocious self-flagellation with a chain. Again, in acceptance of herself and her impotence Chantal de Clergerie, the holy young girl who accom-

plishes the redemption of the non-believing priest of *L'Imposture*
and *Joy*, attains her union with God. The statement of this truth
in *Diary of a Country Priest* as the author closes his journal is
striking:

Yet if all pride were dead in us, the real grace of graces would be to
love ourselves, humbly, just as we might love any suffering member of
the body of Jesus Christ.

Blanche de la Force has to learn this truth through the humiliating necessities brought about by her fearsome nature. The
hatred of self is at the root of the madness which drives the
Mayor of Fenouille in *M. Ouine* to kill himself. Bernanos' work,
therefore, seems to imply that in order to arrive at being a child
again, man must learn to stop hating himself—for otherwise he is
in danger of hating both God in himself as well as what God
wants to accomplish in man through what He has given him.

As strange as it may seem at first glance, the setting Bernanos
chose for the majority of his novels is of importance spiritually
as well as aesthetically. Half of Bernanos' novels are set in the
wet, woody haunts of France's Artois region, in the *département*
of Pas-de-Calais. There the odors of wet clay and decaying leaves
blend with the smell of the *genièvre* with which the peasants lace
their bowls of coffee, sipped through a sugar cube held between
their teeth. Bernanos' spirituality has a distinctively Flemish
robustness about it which often shocks the more legally-minded,
scrupulous Catholic.[7] Since the local priests were frequent guests
at the Bernanos "château," the young boy had adequate opportunity to imbibe a very sane spirituality from these northern
ecclesiastics. It hardly seems exaggerated to venture the observation that any harm he may have suffered from his early education
with the Jesuits[8] in Paris was probably set into a healthy balance
by his familiarity with a less probing, but equally intelligent,
form of Christianity.

If Bernanos' predominant image of struggling for good is that
of learning to accept oneself, the images of the extensive domination of evil in his world are manifold. The idea of the lie which
one lives is not only the theme in *L'Imposture* and in *A Crime;*
it is also a constantly recurring characteristic of his sinners.

Coupled with it is a curiosity, a desire to penetrate the secrets of others, only for the sake of knowing. The two psychiatrists in Bernanos' work (one in *Joy,* another in *Night Is Darkest*), Ouine, the eponomic hero of *M. Ouine,* and Ganse, the foundering novelist of *Night Is Darkest,* all wish to *know.*

But curiosity does not stop with these characters. Indeed it is curiosity which pushes the priest-hero of *Under the Sun of Satan* to attempt to raise a dead child since he wants to *know* who the real master is—God or Satan—and if all his own suffering has been for nothing. It is true that other, more commonly expected marks of evil are also frequent in Bernanos' sinners. The use of drugs and alcohol as well as homosexuality are characteristic of a good number of his more troubled characters. Nonetheless, the most constant sin—which, for Bernanos, constitutes the "sun of Satan"—remains, however, *knowing,* "knowing in order to destroy, then renewing the desire in the midst of the destruction."[9] *M. Ouine* is Bernanos' most finished incarnation of this very basic human sin which has not changed, according to Bernanos' anthropology, since the serpent tempted the mother of the race by saying, "Eat of this fruit and ye shall be as gods, discerning good and evil."[10]

But the struggle with evil in Bernanos is not limited, in either his thought or his work, to great sinners or great saints alone. By far the most common manifestation of the struggle is, according to Bernanos, to be found in the mediocre.[11] Against mediocrity Bernanos penned many elegant pages in his non-fiction, and this, the most common characteristic of the human race, is also frequently incarnated in his novels. Although never actually heroes of the novels, the mediocre do take some of the more important secondary roles: the cartesian priest in *Under the Sun of Satan* who pushes Donissan towards the aborted miracle of raising the dead child; the academician who discovers Donissan's body in the confessional. Again, there are the journalist Pernichon who kills himself in *L'Imposture,* M. de Clergerie, the father of the heroine of *Joy,* and the novelist Ganse in *Night Is Darkest.* Bernanos felt that this part of humanity is especially favored by modern bourgeois democracy where risk is frowned upon and the most basic concern is no longer honor, but security. Indeed, concern with money and position in life are the primary concerns of the dominant class in the modern world of European civilization, a world that scorns both the peasants and the working classes.

Bernanos' implacable faith in the monarchy as the only hope for France was, in fact, rooted in his sympathy for the peasants and working classes. He conceived of the king as the image of the people, as their protector against exploitation by the penny-wise bourgeois who would run the republic for his own best interests. For Bernanos, France's honor alone was to be considered. It appears also that his belief in the monarchy may well be tied to the Christian dogma of the Incarnation, since he believes that national truth, like divine truth, becomes clear only when it is incarnate. For Bernanos, the king's interests must always lie there where the interests of his people lie, otherwise the king is overthrown. But, in his eyes, the interests of the rulers of the bourgeois republic lie, all too often, where their personal gain lies.

Because Bernanos held economic interests in such scorn, it is not surprising that he should not only look upon poverty as honorable, but actually develop, somewhat in the manner of Léon Bloy and Charles Péguy, a mysticism concerning the role of poverty in the cosmic order. Thus the poor, who are always hoping for enough to meet their immediate needs, have hope, whereas the rich have no need to hope. Again, the poor who stand on the brink of despair but still do not yield to the demon who beckons them, give an authentic image of man's spiritual condition, of his unconquerable hope.

Bernanos' occasional portraits of peasants and lower-class people in his novels show much of the author's sympathetic orientation towards them. The charwoman mistress of the defrocked priest in *Diary of a Country Priest* is, in a sense, a saint in her acceptance of the risks involved in her love for her companion: she freely accepts the almost unbearable situation in which she finds herself and dares even to find a cosmic communion with all of man's misery when things become too dificult. The mother of the second Mouchette, sitting down only to die while her husband's and sons' drunken snores mingle with the cries of the latest-born, can only invoke for the reader, as for Bernanos, "the sweet mercy of God."

In strong contrast to this sort of "natural sanctity" of the lower classes is the spiritual struggle of Bernanos' "saintly" heroes. Donissan, the priest-hero of *Under the Sun of Satan,* Chevance in *L'Imposture,* Chantal de Clergerie in *Joy* and the curé of Ambricourt in *Diary of a Country Priest* provide the primary examples of this bernanosian saint. In the evolution of these heroes one can see Bernanos moving towards one primary goal: acceptation of one's impotence before God. If this struggle is most acutely accentuated in *Under the Sun of Satan,* it finds complete resolution in *Diary of a Country Priest,* having been enunciated in detail by Bernanos in *Joy* where, in fact, Chantal de Clergerie's "joy" is defined as "the certitude of her own impotence."[12]

All of Bernanos' novels can be said generally to turn around man's struggle with evil and his response to the presence of God in him. Whether in the humiliated adolescents, great sinners or great saints, whether in the mediocre or the poor, there is a Pascalian theme through all of Bernanos' work: man's misery and his potential grandeur as a being created in God's image, redeemed by God Incarnate and sustained by the life-giving Spirit of God. And, regardless of where Bernanos begins, regardless of what stage of his character's life he deals with, he invariably causes his creatures to look back to their childhood, as it were, to provide the needed balance to the destructive drama of daily existence as the author pushes them towards death. Thus, it may be said that Bernanos would have concluded that in the search for childhood man reveals both his present misery and his past—and future—glory, that lost glory which was once his in the first garden and which has been restored to him through the agony of Christ in another garden.

CHAPTER 2

Early Fiction and the Short Stories

BERNANOS' first extant fiction was published as early as 1907 in a small royalist review.[1] Other similar small reviews published several of Bernanos' efforts before he finally found, in 1913, the perfect outlet for his work. In August of that year, when the militant young royalist had completed his higher education in Paris, he took his first job as editor of the little weekly representing the *Action française* in Rouen, *L'Avant-Garde de Normandie.* But already "Virginie ou le plaisir des champs," a short description of the bickering between a despairing wife and a rustic gentleman husband had been placed with *Mail,* another small royalist publication. Then, in December, a longer story, "La Muette," was published in Bernanos' own paper.

"La Muette" deals with Madame Romains, a well-known woman of letters, who finds her old childhood friend, a respected but not particularly brilliant *commandant,* thrown from his mount and mortally injured in the midst of a field on the edge of the forest where she had been walking. He exalts to her the glory of his having offered everything for his career—even her who never realized he had loved her.

The following year two more of Bernanos' youthful attempts at short stories appeared in *L'Avant-Garde de Normandie.* The first one, "La Tombe renfermée," shows young M. de Candolle, a future member of the French Academy, in the fields on horseback with a young lady who wishes him to declare his love for her. Failing to obtain this, she rides away from him. He refuses to stop her although he would really like to have held her back. Thus he "pridefully despairs of his solitude."

The second story, "La Mort avantageuse du chevalier de Lorges," is written as a letter from one Baron de Civax to a Madame de Duras during the seventeenth-century wars of religion. The

Baron tells how he killed his cousin who was fighting on the enemy Huguenot side and who had charged him and his horse "in the name of God." The letter further relates how, after the battle, the writer himself went to pay his respects to his cousin's dead body as well as his cousin's father.

In these first attempts, Bernanos' love for horses, the out-of-doors, and a certain amount of violent glory can be detected. But subtler images and patterns are also discernible when one is aware of what was to come after. In "Virginie," besides the whole paragraph given to a description of the heroine's hands—something Bernanos always delighted in describing—there is also a mention of those things "which smoulder only in your brain," a theme later to find expression, in *M. Ouine* alone, in three characters: Arsène, Devandomme and old Ouine himself. This submission to illusion may indeed be said to be one of Bernanos' dominant images when he tries to describe the all-pervading presence of evil in the world.

In "La Muette" and "La Tombe renfermée" we find a study of that militant spirit which would sacrifice everything, including love, for ambition; in the first story for a military career; in the second, for a literary one. The interesting thing is that, in the first story, the sacrifice of the commandant has a certain pathetic quality about it, while in the second story the sacrifice of love is plainly condemned. But the reasons for the condemnation in this second case are even more interesting since it is intelligence and ambition—both to become characteristics of the impostor priest, l'abbé Cénabre—which stand between M. de Candolle and the woman he loves. One thus detects already a certain movement in the young writer to honor the purely human aspects of man rather than to advocate sacrificing them for a nebulous idealism.

I "Madame Dargent"

Bernanos' first full-blown short story, "Madame Dargent," was written in the immediate post-war years of 1919–1922 and published in 1922 in the *Revue hebdomadaire* by François Le Grix, thanks to the sponsorship of Bernanos' new young literary friend, Robert Vallery-Radot, who insisted to the editor that the work had the marks of genius.[2]

"Madame Dargent" presents a famous writer at his dying wife's bedside. She affirms that she cannot die. A long confession to her husband gradually emerges. Inspired by the suspect heroines of his books, she had given his fictive creatures "a body, real muscles, and will!" So it was that she was enabled to understand that the "friend's son" she and her husband had adopted was really his own by one of his many mistresses. It took her three years to gain the courage to poison the child. She also killed the child's mother who was found assassinated and robbed in a Paris hotel. The writer refuses to believe his wife: this deathbed confession sounds all too much like one of his own creations. To prove her point, Madame Dargent forces herself up out of bed and in a last effort reaches the bureau from which she draws out the pearl collar she stole from the mistress she murdered. It was reported that the famous writer's wife died in her husband's arms in the midst of an attack of wild delirium, but the truth was that she died even as he attacked her.

Numerous themes and images in this story will reappear. The last agony, the aging writer, the power of the secret which has been kept for a long time, all find repeated treatment in Bernanos' fiction. But the strongest single resemblance between "Madame Dargent" and others of Bernanos' writings is that with *Night Is Darkest* whose heroine, Simone Alfieri, has the same remarkable bravoura and ability to kill as Madame Dargent. As in the short story, Simone Alfieri will inspire her aging novelist employer, Ganse, with ideas for his books, but also, by committing murder at the end, she will actually intend to provide Ganse with the ending he seeks for his current book. It is interesting, too, that when Monsieur Dargent protests his wife's innocence to her, refusing to believe that she really has killed both his son and mistress, he speaks of her "bad dream." This similarity would surely tend to sustain the argument that *Night Is Darkest* (whose French title is *Un Mauvais Rêve*) is not to be dismissed as easily as some critics would like, since within it lie themes and images as much a part of Bernanos' world as a novelist as were the images of the priest and the humiliated innocent.

Bernanos' other two short stories, "Une Nuit" and "Dialogues d'Ombres," published, respectively, in the May and July, 1928, issues of the *Revue hebdomadaire,* are believed to have been written also in the period immediately following the First World War.[3] As in "Madame Dargent" a number of Bernanos' recurrent themes, patterns and images are perceptible.

II "Une Nuit"

In an exotic jungle setting in South America, a young French adventurer, "born for a career and not for life," whose horse has just escaped him, stumbles on the shallowly buried cadaver of a white man. Attacked almost immediately by a young Indian woman who had been watching him from nearby, he succeeds in binding her hands, then makes her lead him to the cabin of her dying master. She avows that the dead white man was her former master. Once at the cabin, the Indian woman and her master bit by bit present their respective—and contradictory—versions of the circumstances surrounding their presence there. What finally emerges is that the dying man is half French and half Indian and had killed the white man, whose body was found, because of jealousy over the Indian woman. In revenge she has given her master poison which is not acting as quickly as she had expected. In a scuffle with the Indian woman who wants his knife, the Frenchman strikes her, and she goes off to a corner where she remains quiet—and dead, the author tells us later—as the final revelation about the mixed-blood takes place.

After he had learned the intruder's nationality, the mixed-blood proudly produces papers in French, relics of his father, which he wants read to him for the first time. Thus the adventurer learns from a clipping that the dying man is actually the son of a very dangerous escaped French convict. Moreover, the one French book that has been kept as a relic of "the great country" is a penny novel containing "a thousand and one jokes to make in society." In the midst of these discoveries, the truth of which the young Frenchman does not share with the halfbreed, the dying man requests that the young man help him die as the men of his father's country die: he wishes the Frenchman to carry out the French custom of pouring water on his head. Much embarrassed, the young man replies that though he would give ten years of his life to do it, he cannot honestly accomplish this since he is

not in a state to do it. Yet he is sure, he says, that God, if He
exists—that God who came to earth and was nailed hands and
feet by man—is good and just and will accept the fact that the
man seeks Him and commits himself to Him. Moreover, if there
is some fault in the half-blood's dying this way, then he himself
will take the fault upon himself.

The half-breed is not very sure of the truth of what he has
heard but says that the young man speaks reasonably in offering
to take the fault upon himself. In a sudden burst of compassion,
the Frenchman wishes to kiss the dying half-breed, but the latter
refuses. How it is possible he asks the Frenchman, that he could
have let be lost that "marvelous secret" of Christianity which
would have made of him "a little child" again?

In spite of the differences between the exotic setting in that
South America for which Bernanos always had a nostalgia and
where he would eventually spend seven years, and the more
familiar setting of Artois, many images of "Une Nuit" are repeated in his later novels. The cabin recalls the poacher's cabin
in both *M. Ouine* and *Mouchette*, while the whole question of a
de-Christianized France, represented by the unbaptized adventurer, is brought into sharp relief thanks to the blind faith non-
Frenchmen have in that country's inherent greatness. (This particular theme often recurred in Bernanos' non-fiction during the
war.) But here too, for the first time, we encounter the idea of
becoming a little child again—in this case, through baptism. Also
of striking interest is the fact that the last fictional lines written
by Bernanos in *The Carmelites* are already prefigured here. In
this play the chaplain counsels Mother Marie to turn her look
towards God just as the Frenchman counsels the half-breed to
commend his soul to Him. Moreover, in both instances a question of honor—of French honor—is at stake, and in both cases the
honor is referred to God for His resolution of the seeming disgrace.

Although this story is somewhat heavy and oppressive, one can
discern in it, better than perhaps in any other of Bernanos' youthful attempts, the future mature writer. The mystery of an unsolved murder spurs the reader on while an unusual female
figure, the secret of a dying man and the mediocre Frenchman

who has forgotten his past already touch upon the realm of Bernanos' fiction. And, as one knows from Bernanos' work, one here sees the author examining Christianity and its claims not according the preconceived notions, but in the light of his own personal vision.

III   "Dialogues d'ombres"

In this story, as in "Madame Dargent," Bernanos presents an aging writer, Jacques. In this case, however, he is meeting his young mistress, Françoise, as they plot their flight together for the next day. Françoise is twenty-three years old and the descendant of a great Venetian family. Her father, whom she hates, many years ago took refuge in an old château in this part of France—a part that one easily recognizes as Bernanos' own Artois region. It was while staying in this vicinity, looking for a writer's hideout, that Jacques, the illustrious author of many novels, has discovered Françoise, his latest love. She avows that she will bring nothing with her from her father's house, only herself. Her family pride has been humiliated because Jacques forgave her for having used him to avenge herself.

This unusual heroine once more recalls Simone Alfieri of *Night Is Darkest* both because of her Italian background and her search for meaning in life through action. Françoise, in giving herself to Jacques, was seeking humility; she wanted to have someone who could look on her with scorn. Only by giving herself physically to the aging writer, she reasoned, could she thus be situated in an inferior position to his own. On his side, Jacques speaks of her as having a religious soul, except that her sanctity is without object. He also announces to her that she detests herself, a theme which so many times was exploited in Bernanos. Yet he is grateful to her for her sympathy, which touched him so profoundly at their first meeting, since he had, himself, reached a depth of disgust for his own life of "writer's debauchery," the life of a man who sells the fruit of his imagination.

Nothing is resolved in this story. In a typically Bernanosian manner it is a study in character and deep psychological motives. In this respect, "Dialogues d'ombres" is the most mature of these three short stories, though it does not, as does "Une Nuit," include enough action to give it a sense of motion. But the power of the fully-formed Bernanos is present in all its strength in this story, even more so than in "Madame Dargent," since, in this story, not only the writer and his books are in play, but also an unusual woman. Françoise, more than Madame Dargent, is capable of acting on her own, well apart from her companion's life and work. Indeed, Françoise emerges in this story as the more potent character and, through her, Bernanos begins to reveal that predisposition he will ever have for describing the complexities of female psychology.

CHAPTER 3

Under the Sun of Satan

COMMENCED in 1919 after the World War I, completed in 1925, Bernanos' first novel was published in 1926. *Under the Sun of Satan* had been written on trains and in cafés during those early postwar years when the young husband and father traveled about eastern France as an insurance inspector. This first of Bernanos' eight novels is of extraordinary interest for the reader who is aware of the direction Bernanos' future creation will take in the seven succeeding volumes. The image of the priest is strongly present in the hero-saint, Abbé Donissan, but the less obvious but equally powerful image of the humiliated adolescent already is found there too. It forces its way, as it were, upon the author and, in the end, exacts for itself the initial section of the book and provides a sort of catalystic action at the very heart of the novel where the priest encounters the possessed adolescent murderess.

I *The Historical Model for Donissan*

That one may better appreciate this artistic conflict within the writer, it is important to point out that the actual composition of this novel is not that of its final order and that its three parts actually evolved into their present positions. It was the last part which was written first, the first part second, and the vast, sweeping second part, with its incarnation of Satan, came last. Thus the story of the old, dying priest, the "Saint of Lumbres" is Bernanos' first attempt at the novel, and the "Story of Mouchette" rose next to his consciousness as a sort of balance and, at this particular point, as a seemingly unrelated story when compared with the story of the "Saint of Lumbres." Finally, in the middle section, entitled "The Temptation of Despair," the author was to juxtapose the two images.

In beginning this novel, Bernanos doubtlessly had in mind a model for his "Saint of Lumbres." He himself calls his hero, Abbé Donissan, "a new curé of Ars," and it is therefore of some interest to understand something of his model and of those traits which Bernanos' hero would have in common with him.

Canonized in 1925, St. Jean-Marie Vianney was born in 1786 and died in 1859. This humble, peasant priest achieved unbelievable renown during the latter years of his lifetime when special trains were organized to take pilgrims from Paris to his tiny country village in the vicinity of Lyons. To this day his popularity is still evident in numerous French churches where his statue remains the center for prayers and lighted candles. Towards the end of his life, his reputation as a doctor of souls had become so established that he found himself obliged to rise at two o'clock in the morning, spending up to eighteen hours a day in the several confessionals he had located about the tiny parish church and in the sacristy. He worked many miracles, although he always disclaimed all credit for them, saying that it was the work of his great friend, little St. Philomena, for whom he had erected an altar in his small church. Today still, his bedroom wall in the two-storey rectory is spotted with the blood which splattered from his frightening self-flagellations.[1] His body, disinterred in 1904, still intact after forty-five years, is still venerated by visitors to Ars. It is enshrined in the basilica attached to the minuscule parish church.

Bernanos incorporated many of the curé of Ars' characteristics in his hero. The scene of self-flagellation by Abbé Donissan is one of the most frightening in French literature, and at the end of the novel the fame of Bernanos' "new curé of Ars" attracts pilgrims from Paris. Indeed, a very famous pilgrim arrived in the person of a distinguished novelist, a member of the French Academy, who came to visit the village and see the saint. Yet a more powerful element was to be borrowed from the curé of Ars by the author of *Under the Sun of Satan* as he created his first hero, for we find in both cases an unrelenting struggle with the "Prince of this World": Satan, the deceiver of mankind.

The curé of Ars, from the very beginning of his lifelong ministry in the little village, grappled with the malevolent attacks, both physical and spiritual, of the Evil One. His charred bed, ignited one night by infernal flames, may still be seen at Ars. Bernanos seemed drawn particularly by this aspect of the life of the saint as if it were a sort of timeless, elevated element of one saint's life which held as much meaning in the France of the 1920s as in the mid-nineteenth century or, for that matter, in the first century. Indeed, Bernanos wished to convince his readers that they did actually live "under the sun of Satan." He therefore wanted to lay bare how he himself understood the workings of Lucifer whose one aim is the destruction of the human race.

Thus we are given in this novel a description of a lifelong battle waged by a simple peasant priest against the subtleties of the devil. This description, on three occasions in the book, takes on extraordinary force, whether viewed psychologically, aesthetically or spiritually. The first is in the scene of which we have just spoken wherein Bernanos describes Donissan's self-flagellation with a chain he has, in a fit of passionate despair and self-hatred, torn from a window shutter; the second, in the bodily encounter Donissan has with Satan; the third, at the end of the novel, when the old saint is tempted into trying to bring a dead child back to life. Important is the fact that this last temptation is described in the earliest written part of the novel; yet there, already, the scandal of the suffering innocent had pushed the hero to blaspheme God.

II *The Plot*

High drama hardly seems evident as one begins the novel for the first time. The Prologue consists of the "Story of Mouchette." Sixteen-year-old Germaine Malorthy, nicknamed Mouchette, only child of an anti-clerical father who makes beer and dabbles in politics and who forbids religious instruction to the girl, is discovered to be pregnant. The only excitement in this banal situation is that the father of the unborn babe is the local nobleman, the Marquis de Cadignan, a gay country bachelor whose estate is up for sale as a result of his financial insolvency.

Mouchette, believing somehow that her affair with the bachelor marquis is too sacred to admit to her parents, proudly refuses to make any revelation, braving all her father's threats and blows. Following his hunch, however, her father goes to the marquis and states that he knows the truth. The marquis believes the skilful liar. Then Mouchette, crushed by the scene with her father which follows his interview with the marquis, slips away in the early hours of the morning to see her lover at his château. She requests that he take her away.

But as Mouchette confronts the marquis, she realizes that he has underestimated and misjudged her, that he has not believed her capable of defying her father and refusing to divulge her lover's name. This supreme disappointment in her lover is aggravated to a point of loathing when he forces himself on her. She grabs his hunting rifle from the wall and fires at such close range that the murder will be declared suicide.

When Mouchette tries to convince her next lover, the local doctor and deputy to the national assembly, that she did kill Cadignan, he refuses to believe her. Her reaction is so violent that she falls into a demented state and has to be put into an institution. There, after giving birth to a stillborn infant, Mouchette is pronounced cured.

The "Temptation of Despair" is the title Bernanos chose for the second and last-written part of his first novel. We meet there the young peasant priest, Abbé Donissan, in his first assignment as an assistant to the curé of the parish in Campagne. The contrast between the two men is all the more striking since the older priest, Abbé Menou-Segrais, is from a higher background and, now at the end of a peaceful ministry, finds himself assigned such a singularly awkward peasant assistant. Bit by bit, however, the older priest comes to see that his awkward peasant is destined for a very singular vocation and he firmly encourages him as he begins to grasp that Donissan's struggle is beyond his own experience. Thus, when he discovers that the young priest is torturing his own body, he tries to dissuade him from it. At the end of their time together, when Donissan is going to be disciplined by his superiors, the older priest encourages him, launching him, as it were, on his destiny as a warrior for God.

The greatest scene of "Temptation of Despair" is that of Donissan's encounter with the devil. Sent by Menou-Segrais on foot to the nearby town of Etaples where his much-esteemed services as a confessor are needed during the preaching of a mission, Abbé Donissan loses his way in the darkness. After traveling in circles and falling in the dark, Donissan is given a word of friendly encouragement by a horse trader who comes upon him. As the conversation develops, the priest begins to realize that he is actually conversing with his adversary, Satan. After some extraordinary transformations and transmutations, Donissan grabs his companion's arms and draws him to himself in order to see his face: he sees his own looking back at him.

Following this series of metamorphoses, Donissan finds himself once more with the horsetrader. He leaves him at dawn to return to Campagne, having long since abandoned any hope of ever reaching Etaples. His encounter with a simple country man, whose inmost secrets Donissan instinctively knows, causes him to realize that he has been granted the gift of reading souls. Thus, when he encounters Mouchette Malorthy on his way back to the village, he is able to reveal to her all the details of her crime. To date she had been unable to make anyone believe her story. Mouchette runs from Donissan, goes home and slits her throat with her father's razor.

While recounting his night's adventures to Abbé Menou-Segrais on his return, Donissan is interrupted when news is brought of Mademoiselle Malorthy's condition and of the fact that she is requesting that she be carried to the church to die. Donissan rushes out to seize the girl forcibly from her anticlerical father and her deputy-doctor lover and, indeed, he does carry her, bleeding, to the church where she expires. This act is judged to be highly imprudent by his superiors and results in Donissan's being sent away for a period of penance in a monastery.

In the last part, Abbé Donissan, now very aged, has become "the Saint of Lumbres," a "new curé of Ars" as widely sought after as was the first curé of Ars. Thus it is that one morning he is sent for by a woman from a neighboring village in hopes that he can come cure her only son from meningitis. The whole action takes place during the attack of angina pectoris, and the reader had little doubt from the beginning of the section that the outcome can be other than the death of the hero-saint.

Arriving at the house, Donissan discovers that the child is already dead. He is then pushed into attempting to raise the child by the local parish priest, Abbé Sabiroux. A former professor of chemistry and a cartesian in thought, Sabiroux suddenly

casts aside his usual reserve concerning Donissan because he feels
it has been revealed to him that his colleague is indeed a saint.

The child, held up to the crucifix by Donissan, does indeed
open his eyes briefly, but at the same moment the saint realizes
that he has sinned in demanding the miracle for reasons other
than love. One is left to conclude in fact that it might well be
the devil and not God who opened the child's eyes.

Donissan rushes from the room, leaving the little dead body
behind. Weighed down now by the awareness that he has blas-
phemed, and wracked with the increasing pain of his heart condition, Donissan painfully makes his way back to his parish.
There, as his last act before entering the confessional to die, he
spends the morning writing out for his superiors an account of
his sin.

During the afternoon, while the saint is held prisoner by the
hundreds of pilgrims who come to confess to him, the famous
novelist, Saint-Marin, a distinguished member of the French
Academy, arrives to see the saint. Escorted by the doctor and
Abbé Sabiroux from the next village, the notable visitor is taken
to the rectory to await the return of Donissan from the church.
As the wait becomes more and more prolonged, it is suggested
by Sabiroux that they look at the saint's room upstairs. Encountering there the "secret of a great love," they are baffled and
abashed by the scourge and blood stains on the wall. The gay
and cordial good company the three had maintained is shattered
by this experience, and Saint-Marin decides to explore the church.
As he probes about and reads memorial plaques and dreams of
returning to this village to live out the end of his days in the
shadow of a saint, he comes upon the body of Donissan in the
confessional where the old priest had finally expired after absolv-
ing the last of the afternoon's pilgrims.

III *Analysis*

Bernanos himself felt that his first novel was too rich, that it
was rather like a display of fireworks which had the misfortune of
being set off on a stormy night.[2] The novel's power, however,
still captures many readers, and its appeal will remain very strong
for a certain number of those who read it for the first time. If

for nothing but the masterful achievement of incarnating Satan, the book would remain an unusual landmark in French literature, regardless of the epoch in which it was written. Yet, appearing as it did in 1926, in the very middle of the general decadence and debauchery following the First World War, at a moment when Gide and Proust were the masters of escapism and irresponsibility, the book served as a call back to the carnal reality of life, a kind of balance, as it were, to the singularly disincarnate sort of life exalted by the work of Proust.

The linking of the name of Proust with that of Bernanos is not, in a sense, all that extraordinary. Léon Daudet, in writing of *Under the Sun of Satan* in *Action française*,[3] said that he had hailed the work of Proust and now he hailed the work Bernanos, the true writer of the *après guerre* period. That Bernanos relied more on traditional presentation of his story than on the subtle, subjectively nuanced peregrinations of Marcel Proust does not alter the fact that he did, in his own right, reveal himself in his first novel as a great stylist who is just as capable of seducing a reader as was Proust. And, as far as what the two men were trying to say, it is only fair to note that, whereas Proust's reader must either adopt Proust's method in his own search for meaning or else reject the whole as being a monologue which really does not touch him, Bernanos, made bold by his Christianity and by the claims of that religion to cosmic truth, insisted that his subject was in no way limited either to himself or to his hero; rather, it was an image of man in general, struggling "under the sun of Satan."

What is this "sun of Satan" in whose black light mankind basks, according to Bernanos? He defines it as "knowing in order to destroy, then renewing the desire in the midst of the destruction."[4] This is the temptation which seduced the mother of the race: Eve, the first woman, standing "thoughtfully and straight on the sill of knowledge."[5] For, in Bernanos' vision of the human race, there is, in each man, a repetition of the fall as man seeks knowledge, knowledge not to build but to destroy; yet, in his perversity, man renews his desire in the midst of the resulting destruction.

Donissan's sin, therefore, is in wanting to know if God really is in command, if Satan really can be conquered. Even as he holds

up the dead child to the crucifix, this curious defiance pushes him
to say to God, "Who is the Master?" He then exacts in the name
of *justice*—the kind of justice which he, a man, can imagine—
the restoration of the child. Donissan's basic sin is thus seen to
be that of despair, of being without hope, without a simply child-
like confidence that "all shall be well, and all manner of thing
shall be well," as the fourteenth-century English recluse, Dame
Julian of Norwich, phrased it.[6] In his early days Donissan wished
so intently to save souls that he even offered God his own salvation for that of others, "if God will it." Menou-Segrais assures
him that this is not in accord with God's way of working. Yet
Donissan's basic lack of quiet confidence pushes him throughout
his life to wish to know for sure just what is taking place. Thus,
on the last of his days on earth, he utters a supreme blasphemy,
saint that he is, in really wondering, and hence asking, "Who is
the Master?"

The image of Mouchette, of the humiliated adolescent, will, of
course, eventually be the unique one in Bernanos' last novel; but
an artist does not easily arrive at a satisfactory statement of his
creative vision in his first attempt. Bernanos had to work out
his obsession with the priest as the ideal hero through other
attempts, and this obsession had to undergo the tempering provided by certain experiences before it was to yield to a more
universal image.

Paul Claudel, writing in 1926 to Bernanos from the French
Embassy in Tokyo after receiving a copy of *Under the Sun of
Satan*, emphasized the unity of the book as shown in the encounter between Mouchette and Donissan: "everything sets itself into
motion to come to the aid of that little crushed soul."[7] Yet the
fusion of the two, particularly if one remembers that the last
section of the book was written first, is not really masterfully
accomplished. Mouchette has no place whatsoever in the last part
of the novel and, in spite of the fact that it is for an action connected with her that Donissan is sent away from Campagne to do
penance in a monastery, she is, first and last, but *one* of a great
number of sinners who cross the saint's path. Even in their encounter at dawn, she is the second soul whose secrets he reads.

Thus, in spite of Claudel's statement, one is inclined to sense a
certain forced fusion here of the two preferred images of Ber-

nanos: the priest and the humiliated adolescent. His next two novels which, he stated in a letter, he really conceived as but one novel, but which he was not allowed to write as such because of pressure from his publisher, will continue this same sort of experiment. There again the author will juxtapose priest and adolescent, only this time it will be with reversed roles: the holy adolescent will save the possessed priest.

CHAPTER 4

L'Imposture *and* Joy

AFTER completing *Under the Sun of Satan* in 1925, Bernanos already envisaged a novel dealing with the theme of imposture and thought of calling it *Les Ténèbres* (*Darkness*). It has been stated that Bernanos thought of using the famous literary Jesuit, Abbé Henri Bremond, author of the monumental twelve-volume *Historie littéraire du sentiment religieux en France*, as a model for his black hero: a famous literary priest, member of the French Academy, who continues to function as a priest although he no longer believes. What happened, however, is what seems always to have happened once Bernanos got launched on a new character: he dug into his own depths to find the secret truths concerning his hero.

Les Ténèbres was finally to appear in 1928 as *L'Imposture*. Bernanos had been persuaded to divide his great story into two parts and to bring them out successively.[1] The sequel, *Joy*, appeared in the following year, 1929. But Bernanos insisted that the reader of *L'Imposture* be informed that the story was not yet complete, and a footnote was placed at the end of this novel advising that it was to be continued in *Joy*.

As fate would have it, the subsequent volume was more successful than the first one, winning for Bernanos the *Prix Fémina* in 1929. In the second volume the holy, radiant adolescent daughter of a mediocre historian who is intriguing for a seat in the French Academy, incarnates the spirituality of St. Thérèse of Lisieux, who had just been canonized in 1925. As with the previous book, Bernanos again deliberately chose a model for the sanctity he was to give his literary character, and here, as with the curé of Ars, some acquaintance with the model is vital to understanding Bernanos' creation of Chantal de Clergerie.

I *The Historical Model for Chantal de Clergerie*

St. Thérèse of Lisieux was beatified in 1923 and canonized in 1925. Accordingly her name and her autobiographical volume, *Story of a Soul,* must have been much in evidence in Catholic circles at about the time the story of *Les Ténèbres* was taking shape in Bernanos' mind. Given Bernanos' gift of psychological penetration, one can well imagine that he was in no way deceived by those right-thinking, superficial Catholics who saw in this young nun a sort of spineless resignation which was labelled "the spirit of childhood." The story of Thérèse of Lisieux is not one to comfort but rather to scandalize the self-contented and the puffed-up, and it would appear that Bernanos also saw there an answer to his impostor priest's sin.

The last of five children—all girls—Thérèse Martin was born to unusually pious, *petit bourgeois* parents in Normandy in 1872. All of the daughters eventually became nuns, four of them, including Thérèse, entering the very strict, austere Carmelite order. Her father's favorite, Thérèse had been left without her mother at the age of four, and her oldest sister Marie, seventeen at that time, helped form her in the Martin household just as she would later, as the prioress of the Carmel of Lisieux, continue to form her for her spiritual vocation. At fifteen, Thérèse, after much intriguing and many attempts, was finally allowed to enter Carmel under age. Less than ten years later, before reaching her twenty-fifth birthday, she was dead.

What happened within this unusual girl in that short span of time is remarkable. She sought to overcome her feelings of frustration and uselessness within the walls of the Normandy convent by systematically offering every action, every thought to God as a "flower" of love for Him and for His creation. All of this she narrated in *Story of a Soul,* her autobiography, written under command of her two prioresses.[2]

Story of a Soul was thus, through Bernanos, to pass into the realm of the French novel, and Chantal de Clergerie,[3] the heroine of *Joy* who redeems the impostor priest Cénabre, is Bernanos' attempt at incarnating Thérèse's spirituality just as Donissan had previously been his attempt at incarnating the spirituality of the curé of Ars. At the center of Thérèsian spirituality, however, underlying the great mystery of acceptance and the offering of everything to God, is found the awareness of impotence before God, and without God. It is that quiet hope so lacking in Donissan which sustains Chantal de Clergerie as she struggles. And her hope is certain, as certain as is her complete conviction that she is incapable of doing anything except what God does in her. Bernanos tells us even that "the certitude of her impotence had become the dazzling center of her joy."[4] Thus she echoes Thérèse of Lisieux's bold statement to God that she wanted to be a saint, but sensing her own impotence, therefore asked God *Himself* to be her sanctity. This simple awareness, completely like that of the child who wishes to buy his father a gift but is unable to do so until his father gives him the money for it, was therefore to be the answer to the pomp and importance surrounding a worldly, literary priest, an authority on all sorts of mystics, a very great scholar who had spent his life poring over the writings of those who had had unusual experiences of God.

Divided into four sections, *L'Imposture*'s first section begins with a painful scene. The famous literary priest, Abbé Cénabre, is hearing the confession of a mediocre Catholic journalist who has chosen the illustrious man as his spiritual director. After torturing Pernichon with his indiscreet questions, Cénabre dismisses his penitent and says in very final terms that he no longer will be able to see him.

During the night after so cruelly dismissing Pernichon, however, Cénabre reaches an interior crisis so intense that he tries to kill himself; but the revolver does not fire. Saying that he has lost his faith, Cénabre decides to telephone for help. In the middle of the night he summons to his room an old priest for whom he had found a modest place in Paris after the old man had been disciplined by his superior for having—successfully—exorcised a girl in his country parish. The old priest, Abbé Chevance, has earned in Paris the nickname of *confesseur des bonnes* (in French both "the confessor of good women" and "the confessor of maids"!), and he numbers among his spiritual children Chantal de Clergerie, the daughter of the historian of that name.

Having received Cénabre's message that someone is dying, old Abbé Chevance, very much in awe of his august benefactor, cannot at first understand the situation and why he has been called. But once the issue is made clear, he immediately sets himself in the helm by saying that he himself can do nothing but leave it to God. He thus invites Cénabre to make his confession to him. Angered by this proposal to humble himself sacramentally, and made even more furious when Chevance, about to leave, begs Cénabre to bless him in the name of the Holy Trinity, the scholar-priest yields to his passion and pushes the tottering old man down. After Cénabre's departure the first part of the novel ends with Cénabre going out into the dawn of Paris to take the train for Germany.

The second part of the book deals with the fall and suicide of Pernichon. He has been crushed not only personally by losing Abbé Cénabre as confessor, but also professionally since the Catholic literary circle upon which he depends for his work finds him useless to them now that his relations with Cénabre have been broken.

In the third part of the novel we again encounter Cénabre, who had returned from Germany six months before, coming out of the National Library at the end of the day's work. Struggling and discouraged, he goes to sit on a bridge of the Seine and contemplates burning all his notes for his new book. When he finally starts walking again, it is ten o'clock in the evening.

In the Latin Quarter he encounters a Paris hobo, a *clochard*, who asks him for alms, highly unprepared for the long dialogue in which Cénabre will engage him. As the priest leads the *clochard* along with him, he tries rather indiscreetly to dig out his whole past history by promising him a reward. Pushing his pursuit of knowledge—not this time of a mystic and saint, but of an unexceptional hobo—he goes so far in his probing for the beggar's secrets that the *clochard* loses his temper and collapses in a passion. Cénabre turns him over to a passing policeman and returns home. There a letter from Pernichon, marked "urgent," is awaiting him. He tosses it aside without even opening it.

In the fourth and last section of the book, Chevance is dying of uremic poisoning in his sordid hotel room, alone except for the hard-bitten manageress. His delirium is painfully described and he keeps imagining himself going to St. German-des-Prés to try to save Cénabre with whose terrible secret he is about to die.

Chantal de Clergerie arrives and is shattered by the miserable way in which her spiritual father is dying. He tells her to leave him, that it is hard to die, that she has no business there. He even refuses to bless her.

Crushed in her sentiments, yet still undaunted in her spiritual awareness, Chantal then offers him her joy—that joy which Bernanos will describe in his next novel as "the certitude of her own impotence." After some hesitation and just at his last moments, this offer is accepted. Chevance is thus enabled to yield to God's wisdom and overcome his struggle to try, himself, to save Cénabre whose ministration he had vainly requested in his last hour.

The same evening Chantal's father, trying to be sympathetic to what his daughter had undergone that day, suggests that she take the eminent Cénabre as her new spiritual director.

Thus are we led into *Joy*. This novel, however, will move beyond those limits placed by a mere conflict between Chantal and Cénabre; the girl will actually be at the center of a whole household of sinners. The first of the novel's two parts presents the regular inhabitants of this unusual household where we encounter, among other servants, the drug-addicted Russian chauffeur, Fiodor, who knows Chantal is a saint and will eventually kill her. At the head of the house is Chantal's mediocre, intriguing historian father. He wants only to get rid of her so that he can marry a certain baroness who will assure the support necessary for his being named to the French Academy. Finally there is Chantal's mad paternal grandmother, devoured by avarice and the fetid memories of having morally killed Chantal's mother.

In the second part of the book, the household's singularity is invaded by the presence of two house guests, her father's illustrious friends, the psychiatrist Lapérouse and Abbé Cénabre. Both have been invited to the de Clergerie country house for the express purpose of explaining to de Clergerie what is wrong with his daughter whose piety somehow does not include the desire to enter a convent.

Taking us through encounters with all these sinners, Bernanos shows us how Chantal's simplicity wins out each time, although it is often an extremely painful experience. In the greatest single scene in the book we are given a description of Chantal at prayer, envisaging the Agony in the Garden where Christ, while suffering for all mankind, could think only of the one man who betrayed Him. It seems that Bernanos, in having Cénabre interrupt this prayer of Chantal, wishes to underline the role of Judas which Cénabre, with his strictly intellectual and rational approach to sanctity, is playing in the vast drama presented in these two books.

The story is brought to a swift, violent climax, and Cénabre is converted when Monsieur de Clergerie leaves to visit the baroness. Fiodor, the mad Russian chauffeur, enters Chantal's room and kills himself after murdering her. The cook, suspecting something, calls Abbé Cénabre, and the two of them go into the room. His own logic finally shattered, Cénabre twice has the cook pray the Our Father. Finally he himself cries out "Pater noster" and falls. He dies later in an institution without having regained his reason, we are told in a footnote.

It is interesting that Bernanos shifted from a direct conflict between Chantal and Cénabre to a more universal application of the girl's spiritual gifts through such characters as the mad grandmother and the psychiatrist. In her encounter with Cénabre, as one might suspect, the central issue is that of Chevance's secret which Cénabre at first thinks she knows but which, in the end, he himself confides to her. We are thus brought back to the central theme of these two books: the salvation of Cénabre by a holy girl. This basic Christian concept of a saint paying for a sinner, so very strong in the work of Claudel, is thus still strongly present in these two novels of Bernanos.[5]

Perhaps this taking stock of just what he had to say in relation to the truth of life itself and his own personal experience caused Bernanos to consider these first three novels as a "first lap." Abandoning the novel for another book, one he hoped to become part of a whole series generally entitled "France's Dismissal,"[6] Bernanos embarked on *The Great Fear of the Right-Thinking* (*La grande peur des bien-pensants*) which he based on the life of Edouard Drumont.

CHAPTER 5

A Crime *and* Night Is Darkest

THE simple explanation of the time necessary to write a book such as *La Grande peur des bien-pensants* would suffice to explain why there was no novel after *Joy* had won the *Prix Fémina* for Bernanos in 1929. Yet Bernanos himself maintained that the whole thing was more complicated. *La Grande peur* appeared in 1931, and evidence shows that Bernanos did indeed, in the first two months of that year, embark not only on one, but on two, new novels: *Night Is Darkest* first; then, a few weeks later, his ill-fated masterpiece, *M. Ouine*. Yet neither of these works was to appear in the immediate future. *M. Ouine* finally came out in Brazil in 1943; *Night Is Darkest* was published in France in 1950, two years after Bernanos' death.

In explaining something of his own artistic position at the time, Bernanos maintained that in his first three volumes he had completed a "first lap" as a novelist and that now he had to plunge more deeply into his creative vision to accomplish what he knew he had to say.[1] His pleas with his publisher, who became more and more uneasy as Bernanos' account crept farther and farther towards the red, reveal the author's hurt pride at having arrived at such an impasse in his "vocation" as a novelist. True, *Under the Sun of Satan* had, as it were, broken the bank for the unknown writer of thirty-eight, but *L'Imposture* was much less successful than its predecessor. *Joy*, in spite of winning a literary prize, was not all that exceptional in its appeal. Moreover, *La Grande peur des bien-pensants* was a highly controversial book, supposedly written as a sort of homage to the arch anti-Semite of France. Such a polemically charged book, in the eyes of the publisher of Bernanos' novels, hardly reassured them of his future as a creator of fiction, and it is interesting to note that this book was published by Grasset and not by Plon, the publisher of all Bernanos' novels.

The first lap was thus finished, and from now until the end of his life Bernanos was to be subject to almost incessant financial worries and a daily, humiliating anguish as he tried to accomplish what he, before God, felt he had been born to accomplish. This second lap, however, is somewhat harder to define because of its lack of clear-cut milestones. As has been pointed out, two of Bernanos' novels were begun in the early years of 1931. Yet it was neither of these which was to appear when Bernanos' "next" novel came out in 1935. This was to be Bernanos' unique attempt at writing a purely money-making book, a murder mystery fittingly entitled *A Crime*.

This murder mystery, however, should not be dismissed too easily even if Bernanos himself said that for him it counted for nothing. Indeed, one can see the images in *A Crime* of both priest and humiliated adolescent and, if Bernanos does not go as deeply as usual in his analysis of character, the end result is, nonetheless, a purely "bernanosian" novel. *A Crime* is a novel which no other author could possibly have written, one where all the trademarks of its creator's craft are evident, as it were in an embryonic form, with the characters themselves being rough sketches and caricatures of the more fully developed characters in other novels.

The evolution of this novel is intimately tied to Bernanos' personal difficulties as a novelist and the father of six children who had no source of income but his writing. Since neither of the two novels started in 1931 had advanced enough to assure any immediate publication and since the year 1933 was particularly hard on Bernanos—his motorcycle accident in July left him a permanent cripple obliged to use two canes to walk the rest of his life; then his sixth child was born in September following this disaster, thus straining still further an already strained household—there had to be some immediate solution for paying bills. So it was that in mid-1934 Bernanos went to Paris to dine with his publisher. During the course of things they hit upon an idea to relieve Bernanos' financial embarrassment: he would write detective stories in the style of Simenon both to ensure an income and to relieve that terrible pressure of finances which made work on his "real" novels almost impossible.[2] Immediately setting to work, Bernanos completed the first part of *A Crime* the next month, August, 1934.

Because Bernanos' financial crisis was unable to await a solution, at this point he proposed to his publisher that he be paid an advance on his royalties for all the manuscript he sent.

As mentioned before, to reduce family expenses still further, the whole family left for Majorca in October of the same year. From there Bernanos sent a second part of his detective story which, on its arrival, began to arouse the suspicions of the publisher. In this second part, unlike the first, one caught scent of one of Bernanos' "real" novels. The whole situation was finally resolved when Bernanos took back the second part and rewrote it, adding a third part to end the mystery. He then incorporated those pages for which he had already been paid into *Night Is Darkest*!

The two novels are thus deeply tied in the workings of Bernanos' creative vision, and the principal female personage in each novel is, if not one and the same person, at least of the same stripe. Moreover, the crime with which *Night Is Darkest* concludes is the same crime as that with which *A Crime* begins. Thus are we obliged to view these two works not only in relation to Bernanos' artistic vision as a whole, but also in their very intimate relation to one another.

A Crime actually opens with a double crime. On the morning the new curé arrives in the village of Mégère, two crimes are discovered. First, the body of Madame Beauchamp, assassinated by a blow which had broken her back, is found. Madame Beauchamp was a rich old lady who lived alone in the village except for a young maid and a woman companion, a secularized nun, Madame Louise. Next, an unknown young man dressed only in a shirt and trousers, is found shot and dying in the woods.

Interrogations begin. The chief investigator is particularly struck by some mysterious element in the new curé but cannot pin it down. He also discovers that the pistol which Madame Beauchamp kept in her house has been stolen.

Then, in the second part of the book, at the same time one discovers that the new curé has left the village, one learns also that the old lady's companion, Madame Louise, has committed suicide by an overdose of morphine, a drug to which she was addicted. She has left a cryptic note speaking of expiation and ending with a mysterious phrase: "honor to the curé of Mégère, honor to that martyr." This, of course, precludes any thought of her having hoped to inherit her mistress's fortune, and, indeed, the only heir of old Madame Beauchamp is a niece who lives as recluse at Châteauroux.

From the altar boy, who has in this very short interval formed a strong attachment to the new curé, it is learned that he has aided the priest in his departure by arranging for a bicycle. Then the boy himself disappears.

The truth emerges only in the third part of the novel which concludes with both the altar boy and his master committing suicide separately, each without knowing that the other chose a similar fate.

The explanation of this mystery is indeed shattering. The new priest is not a priest at all but a young woman who had been a companion of the recluse of Châteauroux. She had come to the village, murdered her companion's rich aunt and now finds herself faced by the new priest. He can, of course, accuse her, once the murder of the old woman is discovered. She shoots him with the pistol she had taken from Madame Beauchamp, strips off his cassock and masquerades as the new priest.

But the story is more complicated yet. Evangeline, the young murderess, besides being the companion of the rich old woman's recluse niece at Châteauroux, is also the daughter of Madame Louise, the secularized nun. It is therefore surmised that Evangeline is actually the child of a priest. Her mother's whole life had been spent fleeing her past as she moved from position to position, trying to protect her daughter from the unbearable truth. It was thus Madame Louise herself who had finally been responsible for securing of her illegitimate daughter a safe haven as the companion of her own rich employer's recluse niece, hoping undoubtedly that her unfortunate child will thus be able to profit from the recluse's eventual inheritance.

Once she has succeeded in placing her daughter at Châteauroux, Madame Louise never sees her again until the day of the murder. She is thus completely aware of everything and kills herself in order not to have to live through a discovery of the truth, not only about her daughter, but about her own past and her implied responsibility for such an unusual child. It is to be noted also that Madame Louise, through her suicide and note, may also hope that she can so embroil the investigation in unsolved riddles that the task of the investigators will become impossibly knotted.

The murderess Evangeline, after fleeing with the altar boy, finally admits to him that she is not the curé of Mégère. He abandons her after she has confided to him the secret of her life at Châteauroux. In a rather long letter which Evangeline then writes to her recluse friend, we learn not only that there is the possibility that the altar boy may come to see her and that he is aware of her "secret"—presumably that she has a lover who is mentioned in this letter—but also that she, like the murderess, is named Evangeline also! This letter completed and mailed, the murderess, now in woman's attire, buys a paper and goes to stretch out on the railroad tracks before an oncoming train. She is unaware that the paper which she has just bought and on which she is lying carries the story of the discovery of the body of the altar boy who, one gathers, has drowned himself.

In spite of its imperfections, this extraordinary story does reveal once more Bernanos' predilection for humiliated adolescents as well as the image of the priest. In the strictest sense, of course, A Crime is not a novel about a priest; rather it is about a woman impostor, an incarnation of a lie.

Although posing as a priest, Evangeline is at the same time the perfect example of an adult who has been stamped by a humiliated adolescence. That she, in turn, drags down into her own despair another adolescent—the altar boy, André Gaspard— only reinforces the image Bernanos is trying to convey here. André himself wishes to become a priest, and Evangeline, no doubt aware of the true identity of her own father, has been, from her very conception, dominated by the obsession of the priest. Moreover, this obsession was with a bad priest, an unfaithful priest who had used his office for evil. That her mother, Madame Louise, grasps all these nuances seems evident.

The theme of the priest, then, if one admits that it exists at all in this novel, is nothing more than an excuse for a colorful personage, one which adds a certain somber dimension to the story, but not one which Bernanos uses to explain his own interior vision. The theme of the humiliated adolescent, however, is the essential one explaining both Evangeline and André Gaspard. Moreover, if one can imagine the circumstances surrounding Madame Louise's fall, one can well envisage her as a sort of Mouchette in nun's habit, seduced and then abandoned by some sort of ecclesiastical Marquis de Cadignan, an impostor priest. The vision of Bernanos thus tends to remain constant as he tries to work out ways to express it, even when the task he has set himself is nothing more elevated than a money-making detective story.

The first novel which Bernanos undertook after *Joy* was *Night Is Darkest.* He began it in 1931, and it was completed in 1935 after *A Crime.* With *A Crime* it shares, as has just been shown, a certain number of characteristics, its ending providing the point of departure. Because of a friend's unfavorable comments, *Night Is Darkest* was not, by Bernanos' own choice, brought out during his lifetime. Perhaps it was too intimately tied to *A Crime* in the author's mind, too much a part of that questionable money-maker which, Bernanos affirmed, counted for nothing in his eyes. In 1950, two years following Bernanos' death, Albert Béguin carefully sought to ensure as good an edition as possible of the last-published of Bernanos' novels. He took the trouble to see—unlike so many critics—that this work was indeed, much more than *A Crime,* a part of Bernanos' whole artistic vision and was in no way apart from the novelist's efforts shown in *L'Imposture* and *M. Ouine.*[3]

M. Ouine, was, of course, begun only a few weeks after *Night Is Darkest,* and certain common characteristics, certain preconceptions of the novelist are expressed in both books. But just as *Night Is Darkest* was to open out onto *M. Ouine,* so, in turn, *M. Ouine* was to open out onto the famous *Diary of a Country Priest.*[4] These interesting facts of chronology are important, yet they are often forgotten since, in order of publication, *Night Is Darkest* was the last to appear. Yet it does belong, as we have just seen, to that first period of Bernanos' "second lap" as a novelist. It should thus be viewed as a part of that more extensive effort Bernanos was trying to make in his last five novels to show us the "sun of Satan" as well as the "joy" of God's sweet mercy.

This more extensive effort indeed followed the somewhat more confined one we have studied in Bernanos' first lap when he wrote his first three novels: *Under the Sun of Satan, L'Imposture* and *Joy*. Whereas in these three novels his vision tends to be limited primarily to individuals redeeming individual sinners, Bernanos now attempts to rise to a higher, more ambitious revelation: he wishes to show us society as a whole and the effects of grace and the satanic sun on it. This attempt becomes clearer and clearer as we progress in our analysis of the three novels following *Night Is Darkest*.

For the moment it suffices to say that since the general direction Bernanos had chosen was that of studying society as a whole, it is not surprising that *Night Is Darkest* does not have a clearly defined hero. There are principal characters and, indeed, a principal female character who dominates the whole ending of the book. No one hero is truly at the heart of the structure of the plot, however, since Bernanos himself said that he was trying to show us beings who had lost all reason to live, the rejects of older generations and the abortion of the new ones which, the author maintained, were all one saw at that time (1935) if one knew how to look.[5]

If no single character is at the heart of the plot of *Night Is Darkest*, there is nonetheless one character around whom the other characters are arranged: Ganse, an aging novelist who has almost written himself out. His secretary is Simone Alfieri, whom he would be pleased to be able to claim as his mistress. She is a strange widow who provides him with the central figure of his present novel, entitled *Evangéline*, for which he is seeking an ending. In his entourage are also his nephew Philippe and Philippe's friend, Olivier Mainville, both of whom represent for the old master raw material for his novels.

Mainville, a young man from the provinces who has been dazzled by the glory of working in Paris as an assistant to a famous novelist, has become Simone Alfieri's lover. As the novel begins, however, he is becoming somewhat disillusioned with Ganse. This disillusionment is, in fact, the first matter put before the reader since the book begins with a long letter written by Mainville to his one surviving relative, an old, very wealthy aunt, with whom he had lived some time in the past. From this letter we learn a great deal of the atmosphere dominating the household of Ganse.

As the characters begin to take their places, we meet Ganse's psychiatrist, Dr. Lipotte, who strongly resembles Monsieur de Clergerie's psychiatrist friend La Pérouse in *Joy*. Philippe, Ganse's nephew, has fallen in with a group of Parisian Communists. In their political idealism he finds the opium he needs to assuage that frustrated disillusionment peculiar to those young men who came of age immediately after the First World War had shattered Europe's self-confidence and her blind naïve faith in progress and the goodness of science. Olivier is also a part of the "expiatory generation" and he, too, seeks opium, only his is of a more literal sort: he partakes of drugs in the company of his mistress, Madame Alfieri.

In one of the novel's best scenes we are given the dialogue between the two young men, a dialogue on the meaning of those who died in the war, on the meaning of the war itself and of the emptiness of society following such a catastrophe. The scene ends with Philippe shooting himself before Olivier Mainville's eyes since the latter will not openly avow that he does not believe Philippe to be a coward.

The second and last part of the novel consists of a description of Simone Alfieri's attempt both to give an ending to Ganse's novel about her and to enrich her lover. At the end of the first part, Olivier had fled her the evening of Philippe's suicide. Now Simone prepares her dramatic adventure with cold and skillful lying. She will murder her lover's old aunt; she knows all the details of the old woman's life and habits from her many conversations with Olivier, including the fact that the old lady's companions go out at certain hours. This means that Simone can profit from the absence of the companions; she can commit the murder and escape without difficulty or suspicion. Taking her drugs and the syringe with which she administers them, Simone makes her way haphazardly towards her final destination.

Surrounding herself with a mass of lies to throw off any idea of who she really is, she casts herself into her role of impostor. As she nears her goal, Simone stops in an establishment near the village where the old aunt lives. Passing herself off as a traveling saleswoman, she even goes so far as to simulate placing long-distance telephone calls in connection with her business. Having convinced the manageress of the establishment of her authenticity, Simone succeeds in borrowing a bicycle and departs.

But an unexpected encounter awaits her en route. A young priest, newly arrived in the area, joins her. Simone launches into a new lie about her identity and just what she is doing there. Leaving the priest, she goes to the old aunt's house. Everything goes off as she had anticipated: the old woman has been left alone by her companions; Simone goes in and kills her by hitting her with an andiron. She is finally able to leave the villa after eluding the two women companions who have returned and who then retire, believing their mistress asleep.

As Simone flees the town, however, to her astonishment and surprise she again encounters the same young priest. He thus will know that she lied to him about her reasons for being in the village and where she was going and, in any case, can accuse her, once the murder is discovered.

Bernanos leaves the whole resolution of the issue in the air, stating only that Simone recognized that she had only one chance left her: admitting her defeat.

Even though *A Crime* begins after the murder of both a rich woman and a priest, there seems no reason to suppose that Bernanos does, in fact, intend for Simone Alfieri to murder the priest she meets at the end of *Night Is Darkest*. Too much effort has been expended by the author in arousing our sympathy for this extraordinary woman. It does not, therefore, seem an exaggeration to suppose that Bernanos offers us some hope for her redemption at the end as she recognizes that admitting her defeat is the only chance left her. Indeed, throughout the novel we have been prepared for something such as this. Bernanos has taken great pains to elaborate on Simone Alfieri's past, on her predilection for priests she has known in her past, and of how nearly she has come to conversion prior to the epoch in which we find her in the novel. He also underlines her obsessive hatred of self.

There are many scenes and many points of interest in *Night Is Darkest* which have nothing to do with Simone Alfieri, so that one cannot, therefore, proclaim her the undisputed heroine of the novel. Nevertheless, only at the end, when she begins her flight, does Bernanos' departure into that wondrous world of his artistic

vision become evident and his description flow uninterrupted-
ly. Ganse is left behind as is Olivier Mainville. Only Simone
seems to count, and it would appear that in the author's eyes it
is only her redemption, her admission of defeat which truly
matters in the whole novel. Hence the strange, rather ambiguous
ending which can probably be understood if one bear in mind
the general, repeated patterns used by Bernanos.

Where, then, is to be found the theme of the priest and humiliated adolescent? Simone Alfieri, like her sister Evangeline of
A Crime, does indeed have a certain interest—a predilection, as
we have just stated—for priests; again, like Evangeline, Simone
Alfieri suffered in her adolescence. Although her wounds were
hardly as spectacular as those of Evangeline, Simone did not
have a normal home life: she was reared by an uncle whose religious attitudes were not such as to help the orphan reconcile
herself with either man or God.

Another form of humiliated adolescence, however, is also to be
seen in *Night Is Darkest* in the persons of the two young men,
Philippe and Olivier. Both belong to the post-World War I generation of young people who sought their master in André Gide.
Moreover, they serve admirably to illustrate the author's thoughts
on the mystery of the dead left on the battlefields of Europe,
giving thereby a larger, vaster application of the central image of
humiliated adolescent.

As for Ganse, he is the brother of Cénabre, a continuation of
that rather unhealthy probing that Bernanos made of the darker
side of his own interior life. With Cénabre Bernanos had attempted to dissect the whole issue of lying and hypocrisy; with
Ganse it is the revelation of a novelist at a dead end, of a frustrated man trying to produce by means of a certain parasitical
feeding on those around him or, worse yet, on his own childhood.
A very close parallel exists with Bernanos' early short story,
"Madame Dargent," wherein we are also shown a writer who fed
on those around him.

One of the book's most beautiful moments is that in which
Simone Alfieri acts as a sort of voice of conscience for Ganse; he
says that he will write a book about his childhood and tell everything—all those things no one ever dares tell about childhood—
his secretary, however, counsels him to keep these secrets sacred

and to himself; if they cannot help him to live, they surely can help him die.

Thus, if the theme of the priest is more or less relegated to certain interior dispositions of Simone Alfieri and to the apparition of a country priest at the end, the theme of childhood and of humiliated adolescence is present as a motivating force in all four of the books' main characters.

It is interesting, of course, that it is Simone Alfieri and not Ganse who finally wins out in the end as the stronger character. Yet it is only an indication of Bernanos' preference for the female as a central figure in his work. Indeed, if it can be said that the adolescent is, by definition, more female than male, Bernanos can be seen to have been overwhelmingly obsessed with the psychology of woman. Male figures such as Donissan and Cénabre do exist; in a character such as Ganse, however, the adolescent is still very much alive, and through such a foil as Dr. Lipotte, Bernanos is enabled to describe and probe this adolescent nature extensively.

CHAPTER 6

Diary of a Country Priest *and* Mouchette

N O novel of Bernanos has enjoyed such unreserved acclaim
as his *Diary of a Country Priest*. In 1934 this novel had
taken shape in the author's mind as he described another country
priest, the curé of Fenouille in *M. Ouine*. The young priest to be
found in *M. Ouine* is thus to be viewed as a first sketch for the
singular young hero of the *Diary*.[1]

The writing of *Diary of a Country Priest* is remarkable on
several counts. Self-evident is the unity of narration: the whole
story is told in the first person, thanks to the journal form. Only
a brief letter affixed at the end to describe the young hero's death
breaks that singleness of vision into which the reader is caught
up from the first lines: "My parish is a parish like the others."
But another, less evident unity, rooted in the chronology of Bernanos' work, undoubtedly has contributed largely to making the
book the masterpiece it is: this is its relative unity of composition.

Unlike the other three novels begun before it in this "second
lap," *Diary of a Country Priest* suffered only one interruption
during the course of its composition. At Christmas, 1934, Bernanos mentioned in a letter that he had begun a new novel. Work
on this new novel continued until February. Then the author was
obliged to turn his attention to rewriting the second and, as it
turned out, to adding a third part to *A Crime*. The first version of
this second part, let us recall, had aroused the suspicion of the
publisher. After all, he wanted only a detective story that would
sell. On completion of the new version of the second (and the
new third) part of *A Crime*, in May, 1935, Bernanos decided to
complete also *Night Is Darkest* before returning to *Diary of a
Country Priest*. The reason, as has already been pointed out,[2]
was that Bernanos intended to use the rejected second part of
A Crime in his story of Simone Alfieri. His scrupulousness in

giving his publisher full measure for those pages for which he had already been paid is, in the circumstances, quite striking.

In September, 1935, after he had rewritten the whole second and the new third part of *A Crime* and after he had completed *Night Is Darkest,* Bernanos returned to *Diary of a Country Priest,* abandoned the previous February. By January, 1936, the book was completed. On its appearance two months later, the immediate success of *Diary of a Country Priest* surpassed even the spectacular achievement of *Under the Sun of Satan,* and the French Academy awarded it its *Grand Prix du Roman.*

As for the author's attitude towards *Diary,* we know that Bernanos set great store by it. Shortly after he had begun this novel, Bernanos stated that he thought it possible that he had never, to date, achieved such firmness and such tenderness.[3] He avowed also, as he was embarking on the second phase of writing the novel in September, 1935, that he loved that book as if he himself had not written it, that he did not love his other novels: *Under the Sun of Satan, L'Imposture* and *Joy.* (It is interesting to note that he passes over *A Crime* in complete silence![4]) He also wrote in November, 1936, after *Diary* had appeared in March, that he had often dreamed, in writing it, of keeping it for himself, of sticking the manuscript in the bottom of a drawer so as to delight his friends after his death. (Just such a fate was indeed to await his last work of fiction: *The Carmelites.*) But, as Bernanos observed in referring to the *Diary:* "Alas! our books belong to us as little as do our lives!"[5]

I Diary of a Country Priest

A serious, very intense young priest (in Bernanos' mind, no doubt, that same nameless figure which appeared not only in *M. Ouine,* but also in *A Crime* and in *Night Is Darkest*), fresh from the seminary and only recently ordained, announces in the first lines of the journal he has decided to keep that he has observed that his parish is devoured by boredom. It is a cancer feeding on the very life of the parish, nourishing itself until it destroys its source of sustenance and itself as well. This image of cancer to represent the presence of evil, brought into play from the very first page of the novel, will remain dominant throughout the book: it is a cancer of the stomach, it will be revealed, which is actually devouring the life of the young priest.

To relieve the limited perspective afforded by the insights of an inexperienced young cleric, Bernanos introduces an older priest in a neighboring village. The curé of Torcy befriends his young colleague and, through his solid, healthy and down-to-earth spirituality, serves as a sort of spokesman for the author himself.

The curé of Torcy, in fact, is a man of great depth. In his youth he had passed through a great crisis and had even contemplated suicide, but now he has arrived at an astounding degree of compassionate understanding and acceptance. His wisdom, so in contrast to the naïveté of the young curé of Ambricourt, is nowhere better illustrated than in the example he chooses when he tries to convince his young friend that the Church is a family house and that one is wrong to expect it to be without spot.

In this connection, the curé of Torcy narrates the anecdote of a former nun he had as his sacristan. She was so determined that the house of God should be immaculate and she worked so hard scrubbing floors after the troop of peasants had poured in that she killed herself from overwork. The curé of Torcy is quite willing to say that she was a martyr in a certain sense; her fault, however, had been that she wished to annihilate dirt instead of being content to fight it. So, he reasons, God intends that man regard the presence of evil as a presence to be combatted but not eradicated, since that is not in man's power.

Supported by such a sane, balanced mentor, the young priest jogs along a rather rough route in running his village parish. When little Séraphita Dumouchel looks at him very intently during catechism, he asks her afterwards if it is because she longs to receive the Lord in her first Communion. The young priest is completely unprepared and crushed when Séraphita later says that she likes to look at his beautiful eyes. Whence a scene with Madame Dumouchel. And there are other failures: the young priest's attempts at organizing a sporting club prove completely abortive; his inability to digest his food and his habit of eating only bread dipped in wine causes tongues to wag and merits for him the accusation of being a secret drinker.

At the center of the novel's intrigue, however, are the inhabitants of the village's château: the count and countess, their adolescent daughter, Chantal, and Chantal's governess and teacher, Mademoiselle Louise. This latter, we gradually learn, is also the count's present mistress. By conversations with both Chantal and Mademoiselle Louise the young curé is, bit by bit, made aware of the difficulties involved in this complex situation. Only when he goes to see the Countess herself does the whole ugly center of the drama become visible. The curé learns that the countess has hated God as well as her husband and daughter since the death of her infant son; she has, as it were, walled herself about with despair. The present difficulty has come from the fact that Chantal, whose whole identity had been with her father, has discovered the truth about his relationship with Mademoiselle Louise and has rebelled against all authority.

In a long scene with the countess, the priest finds himself inspired with inexplicably provoking remarks which open up the situation and reveal all the woman's personal bitterness towards God. He finally succeeds in getting her to pray "Thy kingdom come" when he explains that it is also the kingdom of her tiny son. As it were a symbol of her acceptation and a renouncement of her despair, the countess tears off her medallion, containing a wisp of her dead child's hair, and throws it into the fire. (One immediately recalls a parallel in *Joy* where Chantal de Clergerie prepared her grandmother for a peaceful death by wrenching away from her her avarice, symbolized by her bunch of old keys.) Following the priest's departure, the countess writes a letter to him to express her gratitude and to say that she is at peace.

Everything, however, is compromised in this supposed conversion when the countess is found dead the next morning from a heart attack. Moreover, Chantal, her daughter, has overheard some of the more heated parts of the conversation when voices had been raised. She thus accuses the priest to her father of having provoked too great a strain on her mother.

Because the curé of Ambricourt had referred, early in his journal, to hemorrhages, he reveals from page to page that his physical condition is deteriorating. He finally decides to see a specialist in Lille to whom he has been referred. He will also, he decides, use the occasion to call upon a former classmate, Dufréty, who has abandoned the priesthood. Judging by the letters which he continues to send the curé of Ambricourt, Dufréty appears to have married a nurse.

Once in Lille, however, the young priest of Ambricourt mistakes the name of a practitioner for that of the specialist. In this way he learns the nature of his illness—cancer of the stomach—from an unfortunate, drug-addicted practitioner. Crushed, alone and terribly afraid, the young curé goes to Dufréty's where he again hemorrhages and loses consciousness. Arousing, he finds himself in the presence of a pathetic little charwoman. He soon learns that she is hardly the nurse of whom Dufréty had spoken, though she is, indeed, the defrocked priest's companion. This moving portrait of a defenseless, poor woman of the people in love with a mediocre, defrocked priest, is one of the most eloquent pages in all of Bernanos, and the description she gives of her mystic communion with all of suffering humanity could have been written only by a very great master.

So it is that the pathetic young curé of Ambricourt, a failure as a parish priest in his village, is destined to die in the sordid quarters of a renegade cleric. His last words, reported by Dufréty in a pretentious-sounding letter addressed to the curé of Torcy, are a quotation from St. Thérèse of Lisieux: "Everything is grace" (so wrongly translated as "grace is everywhere" by Pamela Morris). He had uttered these words when Dufréty expressed his regrets that the priest he had summoned to administer the last sacraments had not yet come.

II *Analysis*

The quotation "Everything is grace" is indeed a perfect conclusion to *Diary of a Country Priest*, the "success" of whose hero is so questionable. Even the young curé's conversion of the countess is, as we have seen, highly compromised in the eyes of the world, and his whole few months of ministry in the village are thus outwardly, at least, a complete failure. Yet Bernanos, in adopting the spiritual certitude of his beloved little Thérèse of Lisieux, wishes to show that the success which counts in the eyes of God is not what the world seeks.

The truth of this latter statement is underlined in the last paragraph of the curé of Ambricourt's journal, found just before the letter of Dufréty at the end of the book. This last paragraph also may be said to contain an important key to all of Bernanos' work. In it the dying young man speaks of a resolution which applies not only to his own struggle, but also to the terrible struggles of Donissan and of Cénabre, a struggle so frequently described in Bernanos that one feels that its roots themselves must be deeply entrenched in the author's own interior life: the hatred and scorn of self. Yet how smoothly, how naturally does the curé d'Ambricourt at the end of his journal resolve what all the flagellations of Donissan, all the prideful probings of Cénabre could never resolve: "It is easier than you think to hate yourself. To forget yourself—that is grace. Yet, if all pride were dead in us, the real grace of graces would be to love ourselves humbly, just as we might love any suffering member of the body of Jesus Christ."[6]

Indeed, the whole novel seeks to show how this sick young priest overcomes his resentment of his own limitations, of his stupidities and of his own failure to accept himself and the presence of God in him. "God does not want us to touch His justice," the curé of Torcy wisely observes, and an awareness of this other dimension—that of the *mystery* of God's justice—is necessary to see anything in this book other than a sad, moving story of a doomed young priest.

Interestingly, too, although *Diary of a Country Priest* surely has given much support to the popular idea that Bernanos is primarily a novelist who wrote about priests, the dominant theme of humiliated adolescence is even here powerfully present. Chantal is certainly an image of it. Moreover, we learn, the hero himself was early introduced, in the lower-class milieu where he was reared, to the sins of the race when, as a silent, suffering observer in his aunt's country bar, he noted the lustful glances the men gave the serving girl.

But this priest's humiliation goes even deeper. Within his blood is the taste for alcohol, and his singular nourishment of bread dipped in wine is thus tied to circumstances beyond his own formation. Moreover, reared without a father by a poor mother who had supported him as best she could, he has always been alone, and his days at the seminary as he prepared for the priesthood seem, from what he says of them, bereft of consolation.

We are thus faced with a singular, solitary peasant priest who has suffered much in a miserable childhood. Coming from a long line of heavy drinkers, he is unwisely, perhaps, put in charge of a country parish. Yet, given even all these heavy disadvantages, God draws from this singularly unworthy and unpromising servant glory for Himself. For, as Bernanos stated towards the end of his life, when we accept ourselves humbly—accepting that we are creatures and not the creator of our destinies—the mystery of creation is accomplished in us, and we find ourselves at the very heart of God's secret, becoming thereby sons of God and saints.[7]

In a certain perspective, therefore, *Diary of a Country Priest* is a very rare, controlled statement of Bernanos' vision of the workings of God and of one man's response to them. This book's authenticity is far stronger than the striking, hair-raising story of the saint of Lumbres. True, the saint of Lumbres was modeled on the curé of Ars, while the curé of Ambricourt seems modeled on nothing other than on Bernanos' own interior experience coupled with his own understanding of Thérèse of Lisieux. Yet it is just this authenticity of experience which seems responsible for that extraordinary lucidity which triumphs in the *Diary*.

Is *Diary of a Country Priest*, therefore, to be proclaimed Bernanos' masterpiece? There is no doubt that a majority vote would always so name it, and this immediate reaction, sustained by the French Academy, seems entirely justifiable. Certainly, for the best-balanced, best-controlled, full-length novel, it has no rival. Yet *Mouchette*, the little novel which was to follow it almost immediately, must surely be admitted to be Bernanos' stylistic masterpiece.

III *Mouchette*

Bernanos assures us on the dedicatory page of *Mouchette* that his second Mouchette has nothing in common with the first one except the solitude in which he saw them both die. The author states, moreover, that Mouchette was a name that, as it were, imposed itself on him as he began this story of a crushed adolescent girl.

The circumstances back of his writing this last conceived novel (he was finally to complete *M. Ouine* only in 1940) are rooted in the Spanish Civil War in Majorca in July, 1936. As he saw the pro-Franco, anti-Communist forces transport truckloads of peasants to where they were to be annihilated, he felt that this was a true image of completely defenseless people; through circumstances beyond their control, they had been put into a situation which they could not grasp. The absurdity of such a destiny for man, created in God's image, haunted the author, and he attests that if he had not seen these things, he would not have written *Mouchette*.[8]

The writing of this book is thus situated in the second half of 1936, after the spectacular success of *Diary of a Country Priest* and at a moment when Bernanos must have been quite sure of himself as an artist. Could this self-certainty have made possible this book's polished, gem-like style? Never once do we sense the author falter as he progresses in the description of a young girl pursued by a fatal destiny.

IV *The Plot*

Of a much lower social rank than her predecessor, the second Mouchette's father is a smuggler living in Artois near the Belgian border. He is a drunkard whose household of numerous children and a mortally ill wife are scarcely provided for. Nor is Mouchette's unhappiness at home compensated for at the village school. There the poor female teacher is driven to despair by Mouchette's hatred of music and her inability to sing on pitch.

The novel begins with Mouchette slipping away from school the afternoon of the music lesson. She hides behind the hedge and waits until her classmates have passed. Then, in the midst of a downpour, Mouchette cuts across the *taillis*. (A *taillis*, in the Artois section of France, is a wood which is periodically cut back for making charcoal and, therefore, is of stunted, unnatural growth. As the story progresses, this will serve as an admirable background and symbol of Mouchette's whole destiny.) Fleeing before the storm, she loses a galosh and her scarf. She finally seeks shelter between two tree trunks as the water rises around her.

Here she is found by Arsène, an acquaintance of her father and the local poacher. He takes her to his hidden poacher's hut where he gives her drink. An epileptic fit seizes him, however. Full of compassion for this unusual hero who has boasted to her of protecting her from the "hurricane" which rages outside and of having killed his old enemy Mathieu, the game warden, Mouchette takes his unconscious head into her lap. As his fit subsides, Mouchette begins to sing for the first time in her life. But as Arsène regains consciousness, he takes advantage of the situation and rapes the girl.

Fleeing once more, Mouchette arrives home at dawn. She finds her mother ailing and her father and brothers snoring drunkenly while the latest-born yells in the crib. Her mother says that there was no hurricane at all that night. For the first time Mouchette realizes that Arsène has lied to her. In a moment of loss, Mouchette buries her face in her mother's lap and starts to narrate her adventure. But her mother dies before Mouchette can make her confession.

Mouchette flees from the house. With her own eyes she sees Mathieu, the game warden whom Arsène boasted of having killed. Thus, a second time, she is reminded that she gave herself to a lying hero.

Her final encounter is with a morbid old woman, the one who always comes to sit with the body when there is a death in the village. In an act of questionable kindness, the old woman gives Mouchette a beautiful white dress that had belonged to a young woman for whom she had been a companion when she herself was young. This young woman had died while still in her youth. Since the general impression which Bernanos gives of the old woman is a most unhealthy one, the reader senses that, to some extent, the old lady's influence was partly responsible for the fatality.

Mouchette finally escapes with the beautiful white dress. She goes to a pool which fills a former quarry. There she dons the gift dress, wades out into the pool and drowns.

V *Analysis*

The most striking feature of *Mouchette* from an aesthetic viewpoint is its unity. We do not, for one single line, abandon the heroine's adventure which takes place within a twenty-four-hour period. Nor do we, in any psychological sense, find the author abandoning her to describe the workings of another character's mind. The latter tendency had already been manifest in *Diary of a Country Priest* where, as a whole, we are given a more solitary, united point of view than is generally true in Bernanos. Yet, since *Diary of a Country Priest* is a considerably longer work, it was no doubt prudent for the author to incorporate long discourses by the curé of Torcy in order to offer contrast.

Much of *Mouchette*'s success can, of course, be said to come from the fact that it is a very short work—almost a long short story, a *nouvelle*. Nonetheless, through its balancing of image and presentation, its highly controlled and gradual revelation of complete and utter despair and its swift development of the heroine's character, *Mouchette* is a *tour de force* which only a master writer could have achieved. The building up of Mouchette's confidence in her boasting abductor; the careful balance which Bernanos maintains at the awful moment of the rape where the girl is half desirous and half terrified; the gradual descent from this key event as she has to submit to her mother's death and the indisputable confirmation that her virginity has been taken from her by a liar; the realization that she had lost her innocence for an illusion; and then the fatal encounter with the perverted old wake-keeper—all these happenings gradually lead the reader to sympathize with the unfortunate girl's suicide, almost as if he were himself an accomplice to it.

This effect is undoubtedly in keeping with the author's intentions. Bernanos' last remark on the dedicatory page concerning the two Mouchettes is: "To one and the other of them may God be merciful!" This is not, for an author such as Bernanos, a hollow statement. All that both Mouchettes represented—that is, all the despair of man who is faced with evil in a perverted creation —all of this, Bernanos trusts, is worthy of God's mercy.

One can see, therefore, that Bernanos has clearly confirmed in this last novel his preference for the humiliated adolescent as the major image in his work as he sought to reveal his vision of man. The priest, with all his obvious merits as a central hero, has now been completely abandoned. Nor, for that matter, will he be taken up again either in the ending of *M. Ouine* which Bernanos was, four years later, to complete, or even in *The Carmelites*.

CHAPTER 7

M. Ouine

SINCE he had begun *M. Ouine* in February, 1931, Bernanos had always had a singular feeling about this book. Although he hoped that this would be his "great novel," a series of unfortunate circumstances battered down on him. The remarkable thing to the critic today is that the greatness of his book did not suffer from this imposing deluge of assaults: the violent polemic with Maurras and the *Action française* in 1932; financial disaster, the accident which left him a cripple, and the birth of his sixth child in 1933; still greater financial difficulties, the painful composition of the pot-boiler *A Crime*, the completion of *Night Is Darkest* plus the family exodus to Majorca to flee creditors in 1934; the writing of *Diary of a Country Priest* in 1935; the Spanish Civil War and the composition of *Mouchette* in 1936; the return to France and the beginning of his book on the Spanish conflict in 1937; the completion of *A Diary of My Times* and the departure for South America in 1938; all the disappointments and struggles involved in that adventure while Europe prepared for war. All these happenings were hardly destined to offer much tranquility to the writer who wanted to produce his masterpiece. Between February and May, 1940, however, while France fell to her enemies without and within, Bernanos finished the last chapter of *M. Ouine.* Why?

It is possible to see in *M. Ouine* an image of European civilization.[1] It is hence also possible to interpret the mysterious inability Bernanos manifested to dispatch his hero until 1940 as having resided in Bernanos' identifying *M. Ouine,* in some mysterious way, with modern civilization of which, for Bernanos, France was always the supreme image. Thus, until France, once and for all by her own "death" at the hands of her enemies, could proclaim to the world that a whole civilization was finished, the author of *M. Ouine* could not bring himself to put an end to the lessons being taught by the dying old professor of modern languages.

Once published, however, *M. Ouine* was to suffer—and still suffers—as troubled a destiny in its various editions as it had suffered in its composition. Since it was finished in Brazil in 1940, it was impossible at that moment to think of bringing it out in France. Thus the first edition appeared in Rio de Janeiro in 1943. This edition, in turn, was to serve—alas!—as the basis for the Plon edition (and hence for the current Livre de Poche edition), first appearing in 1946 and still the only edition available in a single volume. The original Rio edition of 1943 contained not only innumerable typographical errors, but also two major omissions: first, a page of the description of the villagers at the funeral in the thirteenth chapter; secondly, the whole first third of the last chapter which provided the real key to the whole. Albert Béguin, Bernanos' incomparable literary executor, through a series of accidents became aware of these facts and through unexpected circumstances got hold of copies of the manuscripts dispersed on both sides of the Atlantic. He was thus able to establish a more satisfactory edition which he published in 1955 for a French book club[2] and which was used by Michel Estève in the Pléiade edition of Bernanos' complete fiction.

Even with the improved edition, however, *M. Ouine* is hardly an easy novel for the general reader. There are happenings, indeed: seduction, a murder, a double suicide, a lynching, a man going mad and, finally, the death of the eponomic hero. But what does it mean? A discussion of the meaning of the novel, however, is valid only after a presentation of its plot.

I | *The Plot*

Around 1930, in the village of Fenouille in the Artois, an adolescent boy, Philippe, called "Steeny," sick of his mother as well as of his English governess who insists on holding him and who has been his mother's intimate companion for fourteen years, accompanies Madame de Néréis, called "Jambe-de-Laine" by the villagers, to her nearby château of Wambescourt. There, it is learned later, Jambe-de-Laine's dying husband, Anthelme, has a secret to tell the boy concerning his dead father. The mad Jambe-de-Laine drives her own carriage, drawn by a monstrous mare, and Steeny's mother is about the only person in the village who will even receive the ill-reputed, painted mistress of Wambescourt.

At the château, however, M. Ouine, a retired professor of modern languages to whom Anthelme and Jambe-de-Laine have offered hospitality for a number of years, intervenes and takes the boy to his austerely furnished room where he plies him with wine and ether as well as bread and jam. Taking advantage of the boy's resentment of his mother and her companion and of his decision not to return home that evening, M. Ouine takes it upon himself to dispatch a little farm boy to tell Steeny's mother that her son will be spending the night at the château. The old man then prepares his own bed for the boy, and Steeny, now inebriated, is aware only that he is being embraced as he lies in bed.

When the boy awakens a short time later, M. Ouine is nowhere to be seen, although Steeny vaguely remembers the old man going out in a leather overcoat into the night's storm. Jambe-de-Laine comes now in the middle of the night to take him to her dying husband's bedside. There Steeny is told that his own father did not die in the war but is still alive.

Fleeing the château in the dark, Steeny, in the early hours of the morning, calls on his best friend, the little cripple, Guillaume Devandomme. They converse on the night's adventure, and Guillaume reports that his aunt's husband, the bastard poacher Eugène, had come in from the storm all covered with mud. Guillaume suffers terribly, however, from Steeny's manner of telling his own adventures and is sure that M. Ouine is a very bad influence on him. But as dawn breaks on the two boys conversing outside by the hedge, Jambe-de-Laine appears in her carriage, drawn by her monstrous mare, on her way into the village. A package she has with her is picked up by Steeny and accidentally bursts. The boys see a little brown velvet coat which Jambe-de-Laine quickly recovers as she flees the scene.

Meanwhile at the mayor's rests the body of the little farm boy whom M. Ouine had sent with the message to Steeny's mother. He has been found in a stream, strangled and nude. Highly nervous and uneasy at the prospect of having a murder in his village, the mayor, a notorious woman-chaser who has a huge, enlarged nose with great red veins in it, tells his one confidant, the cynical doctor who is examining the body, that that good-for-nothing little farm hand will cost him his mayor's job.

Jambe-de-Laine arrives next bringing a package containing not the brown velvet coat Steeny had seen, but rather some green clothes and a pair of shoes she says she found. She wishes formally to accuse her lodger, M. Ouine, of the murder. Almost as an afterthought she adds that her husband had died during the night. With the arrival of the little boy's employers, the Malicornes, Jambe-de-Laine's testimony is confounded since they say he abandoned the green clothes while he was working at the château; Anthelme had bought him a new brown velvet outfit which he was wearing the day before. But Jambe-de-Laine is no longer there to answer this contradiction: the sound of the mare taking off coincides with their discovery that she has disappeared.

Thus it is that Steeny, having fled Guillaume, is standing on the road as morning comes. He just misses being killed when Jambe-de-Laine suddenly comes down the road and heads straight for him, crashing in the ditch. Both of them, as well as the mare, survive the wreck of the carriage. Jambe-de-Laine and Steeny get a ride in a car to the château where, in the evening, we see the two of them in M. Ouine's bedroom discussing the absent master while Anthelme's body rests in his childhood bedroom where Jambe-de-Laine has had it carried. With Jambe-de-Laine wearing only a negligée, one can only conclude that she too has now won the boy's carnal affection. Moreover, the boy's bold and violent familiarity with her also serves to underline their intimacy.

The Devandomme family now enters the story as we meet the cripple boy's aunt Hélène who has to sleep with Eugène, her poacher husband, in the barn. Eugène will not accept her proud father's hospitality since he knows old Devandomme scorns him. The old grandfather and Hélène take care of the cripple, an orphan, and the old man torments himself as well as all around him with the family legend that they are descended from noble ancestors. Thus, his daughter's marriage to the poacher Eugène, presently being accused of murdering the little farm boy, has been a supreme disgrace for him. He now feels obliged, in order to save family honor from the scandal of a murder trial, either to go and kill his son-in-law himself or else request his suicide.

Switching to the mayor's house, we find Arsène caught up in his usual obsession of being impure and standing naked, scrubbing himself, much to the despair of his wife. He tells her that they are, indeed, planning to arrest old Devandomme's son-in-law.

Steeny is next shown returning home and confronting his mother and the English governess with the secret he has learned from the dying Anthelme. Thus he learns that his father had, rather than return to his mother, taken advantage of the war to escape her. The reader encounters the boy again only at the end of the novel.

Making his way to the poacher's hut, old Devandomme tells his daughter's husband that he is to be arrested and that he does not want any scandal. He returns, however, without specifically asking for the younger man's suicide. He confides this to Guillaume who, after telling his grandfather that he does not believe the legends about noble ancestors, is seized with a serious crisis which, the reader learns later, will result in his death in the hospital.

But Monsieur Ouine now comes back into the action and is seen conversing with the young curé. The latter makes one foolish mistake after another as he tries to rise to what he imagines to be the intellectual heights represented by the retired professor. On an unexpected command from M. Ouine, the young priest gives over to the old professor a whole stack of anonymous letters he has received attacking him and generally disseminating evil. The old man takes these letters with him, going off to sit on a little bridge at dawn and to recognize that his last chance—like that of Simone Alfieri in *Night Is Darkest*—had been there with the young priest. Then he recalls his own seduction by a history professor when he was a frightened little boy, weeping in confusion at supposed tenderness.

Hélène and her poacher husband having now been buried after committing a double suicide, the mayor orders that the burial of the little farm hand be official. The whole village attends the funeral which, as it progresses, turns into a debacle: before leaving the church, the priest accuses the whole village of being guilty of murder; then, at the grave, the upset young priest slips and nearly falls in; the mayor, when he comes forward to make

his speech at the grave, goes mad, falling on his knees and weeping, repeating again and again the opening lines only; then the
carriage of Jambe-de-Laine appears outside the cemetery, and
the painted woman comes through the crowd up to the grave
and screams "Vengeance!" over the coffin before the villagers
turn on her and mortally assault her.

In the next two chapters we learn that the mad mayor is to be
sent away to an asylum by his wife and doctor. He escapes from
his house, however, and goes to the rectory. There he is found
by the curé who has just come from the mayor's house himself.
There he had delivered a long and impassioned series of prophecies to the cynical doctor, foretelling a multiplicity of cases
like the mayor's once the idea of purity is robbed from society
by scientific "progress." Believing he has safely locked the mayor
up in the rectory after a fairly calm, lucid conversation with him,
the curé rushes back to tell the doctor and the mayor's wife of
his discovery. When the doctor returns with him to the rectory,
however, the mad man has escaped and written in the dust:
"ADIEU." Because previously he had been obsessed with the
idea of destroying himself, one can only conclude that the mayor
has, in fact, committed suicide.

In the last three chapters Bernanos presents the death of M.
Ouine. Chapters 17 and 18 give us some informative exchanges
between Steeny and Madame Marchal, the former village mid-
wife who, out of kindness, is caring for M. Ouine. Since the
death of Jambe-de-Laine, he has been completely alone in the
disintegrating château except for Steeny who spends his after-
noons there. Only in the very last chapter does M. Ouine again
speak to us as he did at his first appearance when, in the same
room, he had seduced Steeny. Again, as on that occasion, Steeny
gets drunk, only this time it is not a seduction which awaits him.
In his drunken condition he does not witness the death of the
old man who has so long discoursed with him on the love of
death. The doctor and Madame Marchel arouse him from his
drunken sleep, after having examined the old professor's body.

II *Analysis*

The significance of *M. Ouine* as a book and of the eponomic

hero as a person seems almost as endless as the imagination and
sensitivity of the critic.[3] Within the impossible and unresolved
detective story we encounter a number of images which were
useful to Bernanos as he tried to express his vision of the general
decadence of a civilization which had abandoned a Christian
foundation. Bernanos had, in fact, thought of entitling the work
The Dead Parish, an idea which was later to find expression in
the *Diary of a Country Priest*. Many have been led to see M.
Ouine as an anti-priest, as being, if not the source of all the evil
present in the village, at least the center of it.[4] A more balanced
view seems necessary, however, if one takes into consideration
the great compassion Bernanos shows for the perverted old man
who, as he is dying, cries for another childhood, a whole new
childhood, and who confesses that he himself knows that he is
nothing.[5]

In spite of the book's title, it is possible to view M. Ouine's
place in the novel as not being at the center of the action since
it is Steeny and not M. Ouine who unites the characters. Steeny
provides the impetus for the murder of the little farm boy which,
in turn, brings the other characters into play. Moreover, it is
Steeny who emerges from his childhood innocence in this story,
as it were another Mouchette, except that he does not, in the end,
furnish any perspective on his future fate, as Olivier Mainville
had also failed to do in *Night Is Darkest*. What is even more
imposing is the description of that no-man's land between innocence and guilt in the case of Steeny. On four occasions Bernanos describes adult assaults on the adolescent's innocence.
Twice in the first chapter the English governess forces her affectionate attention upon the unwilling boy; then Jambe-de-Laine
takes him to the château where M. Ouine seduces him; finally
in the sixth chapter we are given every reason to believe that
he has entered into a carnal intimacy with the mad Jambe-de-
Laine.

It is significant that it is in the first six chapters that the evolution of Steeny takes place. This first section was, indeed, more
of a whole in its composition than the succeeding thirteen chapters. Some of these latter chapters existed in 1932 (Chapters
VIII, IX, X, XI) when the first six chapters were "finished" (Bernanos would rework sections in Chapters III and IV), but others,

after Bernanos lost part of his manuscript, had to be rewritten (Chapter VII and the second half of Chapter IX). Some of this loss proved irreparable, however, since Bernanos did not succeed in remastering the complex vision he had so well begun to set down in the first six chapters of the work.

This loss of manuscript occurred in April, 1933, depriving us of the first version of Chapter VII as well as two other scenes, both dealing with the Devandomme family. Bernanos renounced rewriting these other two scenes, one between Hélène Devandomme and her father, the other between the mayor and Devandomme. Also lost at that time, as has just been indicated, was the latter part of Chapter IX.

But more important for the whole evolution of the novel, according to Bernanos' own testimony, was his motorcycle accident in July, 1933. Afterwards Bernanos said that he would write something, but that it would not be what he had intended. Nonetheless, in the early months of 1934 he amassed his various parts of manuscript and sent off the first thirteen chapters to his publisher. At this moment he also had Chapter XIV well under way.

In Majorca, Bernanos pushed on into Chapter XVI wherein the mad mayor and the priest are conversing. It was at this point of delving into the depths of evil in this very singular dialogue that Bernanos abandoned *M. Ouine*. During this interruption, *Diary of a Country Priest* would be written, and only after finishing *Diary of a Country Priest* did Bernanos come back to *M. Ouine*. After writing a new ending for Chapter XVI, Bernanos seems to have wanted to finish the novel by dispatching his hero. This effort, evident in Chapters XVII and XVIII where we remain at the old professor's death bed, was abortive, however. Only in 1940 was it possible for him to succeed in his decription of the death of M. Ouine.

The violences which this book suffered seem particularly evident in the lack of unity beginning with Chapter VII. Moreover, even the magnificent description of the funeral does not succeed in bringing Steeny into play, and M. Ouine is hardly more than a spectator at the church. If Jambe-de-Laine does represent the château at the end of the cemetery scene, the same is not at all true for the next two-chapter block where we are concerned only with the doctor, the priest, the mayor and his wife. These latter chapters, however, serve Bernanos well as he enunciates, through the priest, a number of startling prophecies concerning the future of the world. Bernanos maintains that we shall see men such as the mad mayor on every side, turning against their own flesh because they will have been robbed of even the name of purity, of any conception even of something beyond themselves.

Of the last three chapters, only the final great one, Chapter XIX, is really of far-reaching interest, Chapter XVIII actually contributing nothing either to the plot or to insights into Bernanos' thought. But in the last chapter Bernanos examines with a rare subtlety the final nothingness of a civilization built on the exaltation of intellectual values above all others. In a highly significant key parable, unfortunately contained in that first third of the last chapter (omitted in all current editions except the Pléiade volume), Steeny relates to his dying master how sailors who resembled them saw a floating bottle in which they thought they saw a secret message. Against their captain's wishes, they insist on lowering a small boat and setting forth to capture the bottle and its mysterious contents. After rowing all night, they still have not achieved their goal, then a wave washes the bottle aboard, smashing it and revealing it to be empty. As the sailors look back, they discover that the captain and their ship are nowhere to be seen.

For all of his symbolizing a dying civilization, however, M. Ouine still does not seem to be incontrovertibly doomed: he does, as we have seen already, recognize his own nothingness at the end and even answers Steeny's proposition, "Perhaps there is nothing" by retorting: "If there were nothing, how would I be something? It's I who am nothing."[6]

It is also clear that M. Ouine, as does any soul confirmed in its own importance and loving its own sin, plays with images and possibilities rather than actually giving himself through love. Indeed, the old master has always had a singular distaste for the carnal—a characteristic rather common with "purely cerebral" individuals who are utterly victims, it would seem, of their thoughts. Having been told that both Arsène and Devandomme were also victims of their thoughts, we come to see that Bernanos appears to lay great store by this condemnation of the intellectual, resembling thereby those desert fathers so loved by the Eastern Chris-

tian church, those hermits who maintain that man's misery comes
from thought-inspired passions, the thoughts themselves coming
from demons.

Indeed, the demonic is surely not absent from this book; yet it
is presented in such a refined, intellectual manner that it can pass
unnoticed, in singular contrast hereby to *Under the Sun of Satan!*
One example of the subtle presentation of evil will illustrate the
point. In Chapter III we are told very near the beginning that on
the old professor's face can be seen an expression of "calm and
lucid acceptation."[7] For one who knows Bernanos' work well,
acceptation is immediately recognized as being at the center of
the writer's whole spirituality. Moreover, for one who knows historic Christianity, it is realized that acceptation can be viewed as
the key to the mystery surrounding the Mother of God, the key
to that mystery wherein she said, "Behold the handmaid of the
Lord, be it unto me according to thy word."[8] M. Ouine's perversion is refined, however, in that he not only knows this Christian
virtue for its positive power, but he has also actually mastered it
to make it serve his own self-centered goals.

Intellectual perversion is the natural result of that purely hu-
manistic view of man which European civilization has inherited
from the Renaissance, and it is at the heart of what Bernanos is
trying to show us as M. Ouine's sin. One the more easily understands why the name of the equivocable master and corrupter of
youth, André Gide, was on Bernanos' lips as he first began to discuss his eponomic hero: he wished to present a man who breeds
destruction through sowing subtle intellectual disorder, a man
who, like Gide, would use his very fine intelligence to contradict
what he had just said. Hence the name "Oui-ne" ("Yes-no" in
French).

But it would nonetheless be a mistake to see in the character
of M. Ouine a simple caricature of André Gide, just as it would
be equally wrong to see in Cénabre a caricature of Abbé Bremond, even if one may, perhaps, permit oneself that luxury in the
caricature of Anatole France in Saint-Martin in *Under the Sun
of Satan.* In both Cénabre and Ouine, however, as well as in
Ganse, we see a particularly dark side of Bernanos' own interior
life, perverted and exaggerated, no doubt, but nonetheless com-

pletely consistent with one another as well as with the rest of
Bernanos' work.

Albert Béguin, the founder of the Bernanos Society and the
author's literary executor, affirmed that *M. Ouine* is Bernanos'
masterpiece since it is in this work that he pushed the farthest
the exploration of his interior world and wherein he risked the
most in trying to create characters to express his thought.[9] This
very astute, measured judgment will undoubtedly remain valid,
challenging future students of Bernanos' novels to renewed, but
inconclusive, attempts at grappling with the richness of the author's ill-fated "great novel."

CHAPTER 8

The Carmelites

ALTHOUGH Bernanos was never again to write a novel after he finished the last chapter of *M. Ouine* in 1940, insisting on devoting himself completely to his writings for France, he did, toward the end of his life, after his return to France in 1945, write some dialogues for a screen scenario. As things turned out, this writing was to become a play, one that would even greatly increase the prestige of Bernanos as an author.

In 1947, Bernanos' Dominican friend, Father Bruckberger, had started a project with Philippe Agostini to make a film based on a story, *Die Letzte am Schaffot,* by the German writer, Gertrude von le Fort.[1] Bernanos, who was entrusted with writing the dialogues, had read the story before the war and had had a copy of it with him in Brazil during his exile. He probably felt an unusual affinity for the German authoress's young heroine, Blanche de la Force, a symbol of man afraid of death. The authoress had herself breathed into her heroine much of her own interior life, it would appear, in those pre-war years in Germany as Hitler prepared for world domination. Little could she have dreamed at that time that, after the holocaust was over, a French writer would in turn be destined also to breathe into her heroine his interior life!

It was this sort of takeover, however, which came about as Bernanos began to write the dialogues, just as it had always happened in the past when Bernanos thought of taking an historic model for a major character. As he always did, in writing *The Carmelites* he drew from his own interior experience, thereby succeeding in making a whole convent of Carmelite nuns as authentically "bernanosian" as any of the characters of his novels. The results were not, of course, what had been expected by the writers of the scenario, and Bernanos' work, completed in mid-

March of 1948, three and a half months before his death and the very day he was forced to take to his bed, was thus destined for the bottom of a trunk. There, after his death, it was found and published by Albert Béguin in 1949 as *Dialogues des Carmélites*.

Presented first in Zurich, 1951, as a play in German translation, it was produced the following year in Paris at the Théâtre Hébertot where it was warmly greeted by both critics and public. In 1957, Francis Poulenc wrote an opera using the larger part of Bernanos' text as his libretto, and the play was again produced in Paris the same year. The film of Father Bruckberger and Philippe Agostini finally appeared in 1960 under the title, *Dialogue des Carmélites*, although little of the Bernanos' text remained in the completely new scenario.[2] The Bernanos estate sued in regard to the almost exact duplication of a title which had been made famous by Bernanos, but the case was lost. An earlier dispute, when the play was first presented in 1951, about whose literary property the work really was, had arisen between the Dominican and the Bernanos estate. Julien Green, chosen as arbitrator, had ruled that the "spiritual significance" of the work belonged to Bernanos.

In any case, it is hardly likely that Bernanos at the end suspected that these dialogues, rejected for the scenario for which he had written them, would so well serve the destiny he had often wished for the *Diary of a Country Priest,* that it be found tucked away after his death and brought out to delight his friends.

I *The Plot*

Based on the historic execution of the 16 Carmelite nuns of Compiègne on July 17, 1794,[3] just at the end of the reign of terror in revolutionary Paris, Gertrude von le Fort created, in addition to the historic names which were given her, the central figure of Blanche de la Force. Through this figure she could show her own fear of death and martyrdom. This characteristic was, of course, shared by Bernanos who had feared death even as a child. Thus are we presented in Bernanos' *The Carmelites* the motherless young daughter of the Marquis de la Force who has always been afraid of her shadow; nonetheless, she requests permission from her father to enter the austere Carmelite order since she is sure that God wishes to draw glory from her terrible weakness. When she tells the mortally ill old Prioress in an interview that she wishes to be called Sister Blanche of the Agony of Christ, it is interpreted by the old lady as being a divine sign. She herself had once wanted to choose the same name but had renounced it through lack of courage. The fearsome girl is thus admitted, against the wishes of the sub-Prioress, Mother Marie of the Incarnation, an admirable aristocrat of very strong character, who, it is expected, will be elected to succeed the dying Prioress. It is thus to this disapproving but remarkable woman that the dying old Prioress commits the care of her "youngest daughter" for whom she wishes to offer her death. In fact, however, the noble old Prioress dies a scandalously unedifying death, showing great terror as she succumbs.

With the Revolution raging outside, however, Mother Marie is not elected Prioress. Rather, a woman of the people is chosen, Madame Lidoine who soon reveals herself as being just as wise and holy a mother for her flock as was her predecessor. Mother Marie thus remains sub-Prioress during the prolonged absence of the new Prioress who, she fears, may well have been arrested in the city. She uses her position to have the community take a vow of martyrdom, something which the Prioress had categorically opposed since she believed martyrdom to be a reward bestowed only by God. Thus, when the Prioress does safely return, Mother Marie offers to do penance for her presumption and haste.

The intervention by the Revolution in the community's life goes from bad to worse, and Blanche flees the convent to return home. When news of the execution of her father by the Revolution reaches the convent, Mother Marie goes to Paris to arrange for the girl's safety. She thus goes to the Hotel de la Force, now in shambles, and tells Blanche the address of the convent chaplain's niece. There she can stay in safety until the next day when they can return together to the community. Blanche says she will not use the address; she cannot go, in prey once more to an innate fear. Blanche does go there, however, when she hears in the street the whole community has been arrested.

Arriving at the address, Blanche tells this news to Mother Marie, then flees. When the priest arrives immediately afterward and says that they have all been condemned to death, the sub-Prioress wishes to join them to fulfill her vow of martyrdom. The chaplain, however, restrains her, assuring her that if God is sparing her, it is not for her to question Him; it is the blood of her honor which is being asked of her instead of carnal blood. Thus Mother Marie, the author of the vow of martyrdom, is deprived of its glory.

At the Place du Trône where the guillotine is set up, the nuns sing as they mount the steps of the scaffold. The oldest goes up first. The voices are extinguished, one by one. At the end there is still audible only the young voice of Sister Constance who had entered the community at the same time as Sister Blanche and who had, early in the play, said that she was sure they would die together. As the young nun's thin voice falters as she intones the doxology to the Holy Trinity, another young voice rises, loud and strong, to join her: Blanche emerges from the crowd and mounts the guillotine behind her sister novice.

II *Analysis*

Knowing that he was dying as he wrote these dialogues Bernanos infused into them a rare personal identity, particularly in regard to the theme of man before death. But other themes are also present. Mother Marie's sacrificed honor can be seen as an incarnation of Bernanos himself in front of postwar France which, he felt, had no honor left and in which he, Bernanos, was ashamed to remain. Sister Constance is also an incarnation of a very healthy spirituality, much the same as that shown by the curé of Torcy; this spirituality is, indeed, one side of Bernanos' own very complex nature. Moreover, the two prioresses, while not necessarily incarnating a personal aspect of Bernanos' life, nonetheless offer his profound understanding of a remarkably lucid Christian wisdom in two different and complementary forms, that of the nobility and that of the people, each contributing admirably, each necessary to the well-being of the whole.

Other aspects are also present in this extraordinary "spiritual testament" of Bernanos. The whole problem of hatred of self is, in Blanche de la Force, again studied and resolved. A strong element of Theresian spirituality is also present here, as we are reminded never to depart from simplicity. But the most powerful spirituality present, and the one that is the most compelling, is that of the author himself. Each time one of the prioresses speaks, we can profit from the spiritual wisdom Bernanos had acquired in his life as a Christian. Moreover, the theme of rebirth as a child soars to unusual heights as it is articulated by the first Prioress.

From this work are excluded, however, both the humiliated adolescent and the priest. The only sacerdotal personage we meet is the chaplain who, if an exception be made of his last dialogue with Mother Marie, plays only a very perfunctory role in the work. Bernanos can thus be said to have arrived in this work at a resolution of his own search for a hero. The relationships and rapports between all the characters remain at the same time both very intimate and very mysterious; a sort of spiritual exchange and substitution takes place at every turn.

Finally, the style of this last will and testament is in every way a happy success. Extremely pure, extremely simple, its lucidity is so transparent that only through numerous readings and a very deep knowledge of Bernanos' whole work does one even begin to suspect the tough, hard spiritual—and human—truths it contains. An example will illustrate this. The first Prioress says to Blanche: "Whoever willfully shuts his eyes to his neighbour's faults in the name of charity is usually merely breaking a mirror to keep from seeing himself."[4] Or, another example: "One may count a certain number of real nuns, but most of them are mediocre and insipid"[5] (translated by Hopkins as "most of them are middling"!). Indeed, a whole science of life, a whole Christian orientation can be discovered here by the reader who has the patience not to be deceived by the lucid poetry of the play's limpid text.

The Carmelites is surely a fitting close to Bernanos' career not only as a writer, but as a novelist. In this work he has brought into play all the old themes—dreams, illusions, hatred of self, revolt, expiation, one paying for another—and has resolved them admirably without having to resort either to a priest-hero or a humiliated adolescent-hero to express his vision which so often was intimately linked with these two sorts of heroes. It is, therefore, particularly to be hoped that a more accurate translation of this work than the present English one by Gerard Hopkins may be made available so that the power of this rare text may be appreciated by those readers who do not read French. This is especially important since The Carmelites is surely the most accessible and appropriate door whereby one may both enter and exit from the author's unusual fictional world.

CHAPTER 9

The Non-Fiction

BERNANOS' non-fiction can be divided into three categories: first, that represented by four biographical essays ranging from a few pages to a 458-page volume; secondly, political essays, books written to deal with particular historic issues and situations; thirdly, the compilations—books made up of his lectures, articles and unpublished pieces. As a source of information concerning the man behind the fictional world, these books are essential. Foremost always is Bernanos' sense of mission, his need to "witness" either as a Christian who revealed his vision of man and God in his novels or as a Christian who fought for his high ideal of France as a bulwark of Christian honor.

But behind every witness is to be found the lifeblood of the mortal who bears witness. So it is that Bernanos' non-fiction also serves to remind the reader of the carnal existence of this man who refused to take his own books too seriously. He will never be forgiven, of course, by the professors and professional men of letters for some of his statements about himself and his "literature." Frequently in his non-fiction Bernanos, as it were, pulls the literary carpet out from under the critic's feet by categorically rejecting their set of values. Perhaps this helps explain why his non-fiction is so seldom read. Perhaps, too, it helps one understand why a critic who might devour the whole of Proust will still find, nonetheless, that Bernanos' non-fiction is too great in quantity to be considered seriously for thoughtful reading.

It is particularly important, however, that the student interested in Bernanos himself read the whole of the non-fiction with careful attention. When the author says, for example, in *Les Enfants humiliés* that the much-vaunted "art" of *Mouchette* seems to him to be one of the "traps" literature sets in his books in spite of all he can do, he is surely to be listened to. When he himself poses the hopeless contradiction that Mouchette herself

would never read *Mouchette* and admits that he cannot overcome this contradiction, he is again worthy of the critic's attention. For, as Bernanos observes in this same passage, he was a
writer and literature was his tool, the only one he had been given
by God; but the saints would surely have a perfect right to laugh
at such a poor means for touching people's hearts.[1]

May it not be said, then, that the critic who limits himself to
ideas which have been formed uniquely from a study of Bernanos' fiction will always manifest a certain artificialitv, a certain
contrivance in his conclusions? This is because he will have created for himself, just as Bernanos often accused even his best
friends of doing, a Georges Bernanos capable of being grasped
by his own limited vision: the critic will have ignored the reality
of the true Georges Bernanos and his many upsetting contra-
dictions.

I *Biographical Essays*

These four essays deal, in order of composition, with St. Dom-
inic, St. Joan of Arc, Edouard Drumont and Martin Luther, respectively. Of these, the first is certainly the least interesting in
that it gives little insight into Bernanos' thought. Published in the
Revue Universelle[2] in 1926, the article is of a rather routine sort,
written at a time when the Dominican order was very much in
the forefront with the "Catholic revival" in literature. Although
Bernanos does discuss certain ideas on sanctity, none of them
bespeaks the fervent personal conviction which, eight years later,
was to resound in his short study of Joan of Arc.

The original title, *Jeanne, relapse et sainte*, translated as *Sanctity will Out*, points to the issue at stake in this essay: a relapsed
heretic, officially proclaimed such by the Church and delivered
to the secular forces for execution, was actually a saint. Bernanos
seems to have enjoyed this contradiction and he exploits it to
the full. The much-vaunted appeal to the pope, he reminds the
reader, was completely out of order since the papal legate was
already officially present and his signature figures on the condemnation beside that of the Bishop of Beauvais. Moreover, Bernanos saw a particular pathos in Joan's abjuring, denying her
voices for fear of the flames and of that eternal hell to which the

ecclesiastics assured her she was destined if she persisted in not abjuring. Thus, in this essay as in his novels, Bernanos underlines the theme of the humiliated adolescent.

It has already been remarked that Bernanos may well have wished to reply to the Vatican's condemnation of the *Action française* through this essay on the saint who was condemned officially by the Church. He had been particularly concerned for the youth of the *Action française* who, in some extreme cases, were forced to choose between dying without the sacraments or else denying, as they conceived it, their legitimate king, unable as they were to separate the monarchy from the *Action française* movement. Such cases did exist, and Bernanos undoubtedly identified the seventeen-year-old Joan of Arc, forced even to doubt the validity of her divinely-accorded experience, with such valiant French youths as found themselves outside official acceptance by the Church because of their fervor for France.

While it is true that this work came after the violent polemic between Maurras and Bernanos in 1932, and thus after Bernanos' own dismissal by the master of the *Action française,* such a fact in no way altered the scandal Bernanos felt or the disgust he expressed for ecclesiastical opportunism which operated at the expense of the suffering innocent. In Joan of Arc he saw, as it were, a prototype of pure, fervent youth, condemned for the graces it has received, scandalizing its elders by the mere fact of having received these graces. In a very moving letter that Bernanos would one day write in the autograph album of a young Brazilian girl,[3] he urges her never to become a *grande personne* which, in French, means both an "adult" and a "great, important person." Bernanos reasoned thus since he believed that the promise of the Beatitudes in the Gospel belong only to the poor of the earth and to "children"—the two extant degrees of Christian royalty.

II La Grande peur des bien-pensants

Provided one is prepared to read a book written to praise the author of *La France juive,* the very long biographical essay on Edouard Drumont, *La Grande peur des bien-pensants,* is of great richness and no mean depth. Bernanos insisted that the Jew was aimed at by Drumont primarily because he represented the power of money. This power, the only aristocracy which the modern world recognizes, was not and never could be in accord with the older, Christian aristocracy which was founded on the concept of self-sacrifice for one's inferiors.

Drumont was one of the undisputed heroes of Bernanos' youth. He remained, for Bernanos, "a free man" who had once been stung at some vital point by injustice. Drumont raged against the conservative power of his day, seeing in it the collusion of the hierarchy of the Church and the vested interests of the capital behind the Third Republic. It is to be recalled, moreover, that Bernanos, in turn, also attacked the conservative position in his youthful days as editor of *L'Avant-Garde de Normandie*.

An example of the sort of injustice perpetrated by the collusion of the ecclesiastical powers and vested interests will suffice to give an idea of the sort of thing against which Bernanos—as had Drumont before him—reacted with violence. In 1890 Drumont decided to run for municipal office for Paris. Making sure that no one opposed him who could possibly represent Catholic opinion, he saw no impediment to gaining the support of the Church. The conservatives, however, defeated him, and the heart of the defeat was anything but pure.

Drumont saw his defeat manipulated by the hierarchy of the Church after he had made a speech attacking a recent Jewish convert, Léo Taxil. Taxil, an unrepentant pornographer, had, in fact, merely passed from anticlerical pornography to antimasonic pornography, using the latter sort to endear himself to the Church as an ally against the horrors of the Masons. His anticlerical bookstore now was simply an antimasonic bookstore, and he had even managed to enlist the press of one of the lay religious orders to print his salacious works. He had, moreover, been received by Pope Leo XIII.

After Drumont's attack, the papal nuncio on the very next day left his calling card at Taxil's to show the official esteem in which the antimasonic informer was nonetheless held by the hierarchy. Drumont raged, of course, and, as things turned out, Drumont was right to rage. Taxil finally, when the occasion was ripe, revealed that his whole "conversion," as well as his "exposure" of the Masons, were both big jokes; on the side, his wife had continued to make a handsome profit from their back store of anti-clerical pornography.

Bernanos reminds us that the conservatives and the ecclesiastical authorities were not only duped by Taxil, they actually helped enrich him. Bernanos thus had learned from Drumont that because the conservatives' primary value was their own interests, such clever exploiters as Taxil find in them ready victims. Bernanos also understood that the Jew, with his search for identity apart from his divinely-accorded identity as a Jew, launches himself into the establishment of the country in which he lives, supporting what he conceives to be forces which will protect his privileges.

Bernanos' later and quite open sympathy with the Jews persecuted by Hitler is not here in question. What is in question in *La Grande peur des bien-pensants*, is the extent to which the Jews, having abandoned their spiritual pact with God, now apply their great gifts to mere temporal ends. This question, a basic one for every Christian and Jew, cannot, perhaps, be answered; but there are temporal powers which the Jews, according to Bernanos, do control, almost as if these powers were a recompense to them for having broken the ancient pact with God.

In *La Grande peur des bien-pensants* Bernanos also went far in showing the essential evil of modern society which has been formed by the conservative spirit. This is the society which has created a new kind of misery, a misery the like of which, according to Bernanos, man has never seen before. *La Grande peur des bien-pensants* thus joins the writings of Péguy in its uncompromising condemnation of the forces controlling modern society, seeing within them the mark and sign of infernal powers which aim at snuffing out grace and man's dignity of being created in the image of God.

III   *"Brother Martin"*

The last of Bernanos' biographical essays, "Brother Martin," consists of a few pages on Martin Luther, an historic personage for whom Bernanos had great sympathy. He supposedly had envisaged an entire book on the German reformer and, if the pages left today are any indication of what the whole work would have been, it would have proven extraordinary. In these pages written in Brazil in 1943, Bernanos touches on the question of revolt and reform, pointing out that St. Francis too, revolted by what he saw, also wished to reform. But the difference was that St. Francis, instead of trying to wrest away from the Church her ill-gotten goods, rather himself plunged into the Church's divine treasury of poverty and drew out new treasures whose beauty far outshone that of the ill-gotten goods.

Bernanos reminds his reader with remarkable insight that, at a moment when there is a dearth of good poets, it does poetry no good to hang the bad poets; rather, one must write good poetry. So it is with the Church or, for that matter, with the reform of anything; wasting time trying to suppress the bad is worthless; rather must one heap on the organism those treasures which are lacking.

Another great truth, much loved by Bernanos, was also brought out in this essay. This one is based on a statement by the Dominican, Father Clerissac. Killed in the First World War, noted for his activities with the *Action française* and for being Maritain's confessor, Father Clerissac, in a little book entitled *Le Mystère de l'Eglise*,[4] made the statement that to suffer for the Church was nothing; one had to learn to suffer by the Church.[5] Bernanos liked the idea and, in this essay, saw Luther as refusing this sort of suffering. In spite of his great sympathy for Luther, there is no doubt that Bernanos here arrives at a point of seeing very lucidly the dangers and the futility of any reformer who willfully breaks completely with the immediate past.

IV *Political Essays*

The first and, perhaps, the greatest of the political essays is *The Diary of My Times*, Bernanos' book on the Spanish Civil War of 1936. This war, one was to realize afterward, was but a dress rehearsal for the conflict set to burst upon the world three years later. This war is, therefore, still charged with significance far beyond that of a mere internal conflict involved in a change of government. Supported from outside forces, the Spanish Civil War was a small-scale replica of what happens when one totalitarian force meets another similar force: there is no room left for free men.

Communism, supported by Russia and those of like sympathies, was opposed by fascism, supported by the conservatives and the ecclesiastical establishment—those two forces which both Drumont and Bernanos hated.

Living on the Spanish island of Majorca when the conflict broke, Bernanos saw the passions of both sides. As he revealed in his book, he saw also far beyond both sides into the heart of modern man whose one aim is not freedom, but totalitarian order at no matter what price. Moreover, with the exception of François Mauriac, most of the articulate French Catholics—including Claudel — regarded Franco's forces as a crusade against the enemies of Christendom. The conflict was quasi-officially even termed a "crusade" by the French Catholic press. Bernanos would have none of this. His eldest son, Yves, fought on the "crusading" side, and Bernanos himself knew from within that nothing but terror was the goal of the "whites" as much as of the "reds."

Another scandal, that of the Italian conquest of Ethiopia dating from the same year, was also underlined in Bernanos' stronger pages as he raged against official Catholic opinion. In Ethiopia, as in Spain, the same conservative element with its money interests supported atrocities committed to protect their interests while the Church's hierarchy gave its benediction. In later books Bernanos would return to the Ethiopian as well as to the Spanish scandal.

Bernanos was especially adamant that *A Diary of My Times* appear when he returned to France from Majorca. He said that even if he had to pay for it himself, he would see that it was printed. He held strongly to the idea that at such a moment, when the Catholic world as a whole applauded the fascist atrocities as part of the Christian "crusade," it was of vital importance that one articulate Catholic speak up and protest.

At the heart of this volume, however—the first volume of Bernanos' non-fiction to be issued in a French paperback edition —is a remarkable diatribe against the contemporary Christian. Bernanos imagines a non-believer climbing the steps to the pulpit on the feast of St. Thérèse of Lisieux and telling a congregation of typical parishioners what the whole world awaits from them, the believers, those who have received the gift of faith. He upbraids them for hiding their joy—or perhaps the truth is that they just haven't got any joy? He pleads with them to renew that fresh evangelical spirit of childhood, taught by the saint being cele- brated that day, so that the world may not only be saved from the spirit of old age, but simply saved. Childhood's spirit of joyful acceptance must not only oppose the conservative spirit of cal- culation and intrigue, but must also tip the balance in its favor if the world is to be saved.

Of especial importance in *A Diary of My Times* is the preface. In this, one of the most frequently quoted sources used to explain both Bernanos and his work, he speaks beautifully of childhood and of the language of childhood which he has tried, again and again, to capture in his books. He is convinced, moreover, that the only part of the world that can be saved is that belonging to those who will never read him: martyrs, heroes and children. He speaks also of his whole vocation as a writer, of going forward to meet those for whom he had been born, of how his major char- acters were, perhaps, the true masters of his own lost childhood before adolescence's "suck of death" came to mix itself in the blood of his heart. In the final paragraph of this preface, Berna- nos envisages the little boy he used to be rallying together all his years of despair and leading them safely into the Father's house.

The preface of *A Diary of My Times* provides the reader with an excellent statement of Bernanos' posture both as an atrtist and as a man. A careful study of it is essential if one is to seize the basic conflict within both his work and his person. While stating quite plainly that he is not a writer at all and that the sight of a piece of paper makes him sick, he articulates, in the magnificent style of a very great writer, his problems as he tries to write! What he rejects in saying he is not a writer, of course, is the officialdom of such posture, the decorations and the expected honors accompanying the "true" man of letters. That Bernanos thrice refused the *Légion d'honneur* and refused also to consider an invitation to solicit a seat among the forty immortals of the French Academy does, perhaps, give him a right to maintain his independence from those who take such pride in calling them- selves "writers."

V   Nous autres Français *and* Scandale de la vérité

Both *Nous autres Français* and *Scandale de la vérité* date from the immediate pre-war period; the former was written between September, 1938, and June, 1939; the latter, a sort of short outgrowth of the former, was finished in January, 1939. Both are centered on the problems raised in Bernanos' mind by the Munich pact and the political position of Maurras and the *Action française* in regard to the resulting political climate. That Maurras should sympathize with Mussolini and the barbaric, fiery suppression of helpless Ethiopian peasants indicated to Bernanos how opportunist had become the politics of his former master.

The presence of Péguy frequently cuts through the pages of these two volumes, not only in *Scandale de la vérité* where Bernanos makes generous quotes from the essays of the poet he admired so much, but in Bernanos' text itself, almost as if he had submerged himself in the style and thought of the founder of the *Cahiers de la Quinzaine*. Indeed, Péguy is chosen by Bernanos as a pole of opposition to the position of Maurras and his followers. Maurras was betraying France with all his political machinations abroad; he had forgotten that he was regarded as the leader of those whose one aim was to restore French honor through the monarchy.

The Péguy-Maurras opposition is brought into even sharper relief when Bernanos points to Péguy as the representative of the 1789 revolutionary spirit while Maurras was the representative of that self-interested spirit of 1793, of the masters of the Reign of Terror. The methods which Maurras approved for the expansion of his politics—such as those carried out in Ethiopia—underlined this basic likeness between the eighteenth-century intellectuals and Maurras.

The opportunism of the Church is, needless to say, hardly passed over in silence in these two books. The eternal combination of the conservatives and the ecclesiastical hierarchy, now supported and no longer opposed by Maurras, is attacked and declared neither French nor Christian. Bernanos, in an appendix to *Nous autres Français,* makes a point of printing the text of Maurras' poem *"Optumo sive pessumo"* wherein he detects an equivocable religious attitude destined to make any true Christian shudder. Undoubtedly Bernanos hoped thereby to prove his point that the alliance of the ecclesiastical hierarchy with the condemned *Action française* was as questionable a union as had been that of the hierarchy with Léo Taxil in the days of Drumont.

VI   Les Enfants humiliés

Les Enfants humiliés, the next volume of Bernanos' political essays, termed on its title page *Journal 1939–40,* was completed in January of 1940 and confided to Henri Michaux who was returning to France from Brazil. The *Nouvelle Revue Française* published the first pages of it in May of that year, but the manuscript was subsequently misplaced until 1948. When it was recovered, Bernanos re-read it and made certain stylistic corrections from that bed to which he had been confined after finishing *The Carmelites,* and from which he would rise only to be flown back to Paris to die. The dedication, dated April 2, 1940, should not obscure the fact that this work was the one Bernanos completed in January, 1940, just before writing the last great chapter of *M. Ouine.*

Les Enfants humiliés is a long meditation on the meaning of the lost victory of 1918 and, indeed, on the meaning of the First World War, now that the second one was upon the world. Bernanos bitterly attacks the "home front" as the "rear" with the full force of the double meaning that might be given that word.

But Bernanos' meditation carries him much farther than a bitter attack on the "rear." He meditates on such unusual things as Hitler's motivations and what this frightening master had suffered as a child. And, as usual, Bernanos sees the poor and the "children" as related, concluding this book with a long and very beautiful discourse on the meaning of the poor and on their hope which is so essential to the human race.

Although less fiery than *A Diary of My Times, Les Enfants humiliés* is nonetheless one of the most important of Bernanos' volumes of non-fiction. It is surely not to be neglected by any reader wishing to grasp the basic theme of "humiliated adolescence" so prominent in the fiction, since this work gives the essential historic setting in which Bernanos learned many of his truths on this, his favorite theme.

This book is more "literary" than the other political essays in the sense that there is more of a unifying vision perceptible in the organization of its contents. Nor is it limited by some of the more parochial arguments of the other political books. Bernanos' ideas on the modern state, on the Church and on political attitudes remain the same here as elsewhere, but *Les Enfants humiliés* provides us with a very controlled and carefully worked literary exposé of them.

VII Plea for Liberty

Between *Les Enfants humiliés* and the volume now to be considered, *Plea for Liberty*, intervened not only the final chapter of *M. Ouine*, written between February and May, 1940, but also, with the exception of short articles to be found in *Le Chemin de la Croix-des-Âmes*, a period of relative silence for Bernanos. In June there was, of course, the appeal of General de Gaulle for the Free French forces, then the departure of Bernanos' two elder sons Yves and Michel as well as that of his nephew Guy Hattu. In August there was the move to Cruz das Almas near Barbecena where he would at last find a place in which conditions were tolerable enough for him to remain fixed for the next four years. The first work to come from his new location was the volume now to be considered, a book addressed to England and the United States. Before concluding his "letter to the English," Bernanos had addressed one of its seven sections to President Franklin D. Roosevelt.

Plea for Liberty, in French entitled *Lettre aux Anglais*, consists, in fact, of seven "letters" dated December, 1940, and March, May, July, August, September and November, 1941. It came into being as the result of a request in 1940 from the editors of the *Dublin Review* who asked Bernanos to supply them with an article. The article written, Bernanos found great appeal in the idea of exposing his own ideals of French honor to that "little island and great people" who stood alone against the forces of the Axis. *Plea for Liberty* resulted.

Here, as always, the theme of childhood emerges, and Bernanos articulates for all foreigners the genius of France and her part in the world scene. He honors and admires the English position as much as he bemoans his own country's disaster in the Armistice. When he hears that French soldiers, incorporated in the

German war effort in Libya, are confronting the English soldiers, he concludes that, following the Armistice, all opportunities for death are good for a young Frenchman.

It is of interest that in the "letter" dated September, 1941, wherein he addresses President Roosevelt, Bernanos speaks of America as the nation chosen by God to preside over the future of Christianity. Bernanos could not imagine that America would ever take sides agains the Church, even if the majority of the Americans were not Catholics.

Another interesting aspect of *Plea for Liberty* is the fact that one can there detect a somewhat new tone, that which will especially be enunciated in Bernanos' post-war lectures and writings, a tone of hope that France will once again take her place at the head of free men as she had done ever since the Revolution of 1789. This time the difference will be that the new revolution will be one of the Spirit, establishing the reign of free men and having done, once and for all, with the conservatives.

Quite probably the idea of writing to explain France to outsiders was responsible for Bernanos' setting his hopes on great things to come after the war. It is recorded by Abbé Pezeril how violent Bernanos became during his last days at the American hospital at Neuilly when he saw that American tractors were being imported to build up post-war France.[6] In Bernanos' eyes, France's "soul" could not be built up by tractors—not even American ones! This incident also shows the bitter disappointment which awaited all of Bernanos' temporal hopes for his country, those hopes he began to articulate so passionately in *Plea for Liberty*.

This book thus stands at a crossroads in Bernanos' non-fiction. With France defeated, he had nothing left to do but search for reasons to justify his country and plead pardon for her defeat as he addressed himself to those who had been her friends and allies.

Bernanos' last political book, *Tradition of Freedom*, was written in 1945 as the European war drew to a close. Here Bernanos becomes more aggressive, attacking the *imbéciles* of the modern world on every possible occasion. The themes are essentially the same as in his other writings of this period, but now he shows a hurt pride, for example, in the fact that the French language was not to be used at the San Francisco conference in 1945 to found the United Nations. Bernanos sees therein a proof that the conference itself was simply an utilitarian affair which had no interest in the part of the language of Rabelais, Montaigne and Pascal.

Of all Bernanos' political essays, this one seems the most likely to offend, probably simply because it is a tirade against the civilization of the *imbéciles*. Bernanos obviously classified his reader in that category. The agony of Pétain's Armistice and the Vichy French is touched on here, as in most of these works. Bernanos concludes by quoting President Truman who had opened the San Francisco conference by saying that modern war, if not contained, would destroy all civilization.

VIII *Compilations*

The largest and earliest published of the compilations is the volume entitled *Le Chemin de la Croix-des-Ames*. It contains articles which Bernanos wrote between May, 1940, and May, 1945. Originally issued in Rio de Janeiro as four separate volumes between 1943 and 1945, these were combined into one after the war. Bernanos wrote a very important introduction to this large work in December, 1947, just seven months before his death in the following July. In it he pours forth his disappointment with post-war France, lumping the all-sacred Resistance with the thrice-evil Collaboration, calling them both "lies."

This huge 509-page book of fine print is quite rich, and it would be impossible to summarize it without first establishing a concordance to Bernanos' thought. The articles, many of them directly inspired by some bits of war news, cover a wide range of subjects; sometimes they are purely political, at other times highly spiritual, as, for example, the very beautiful article on poverty entitled "Patentia Pauperum" and dated September, 1942.

Le Chemin provides an excellent general introduction to Bernanos' thought during the war, since it covers the years of the conflict. Also, the nature of the book provided its author with every freedom to treat any and every subject. The one-volume edition is divided into six parts, one each for the years 1940–1945 inclusive. The date of the first article (May, 1940) corresponds with the date Bernanos completed the last chapter of *M. Ouine*. The date of the last article (May, 1945) is only two months before Bernanos' return to France.

Of particular interest to Americans in this volume is Bernanos' letter to an American nun, Sister Marie Loyola, written in May, 1941. In it he expresses his profound regret at not having succeeded in addressing himself to the American public and laments not having found an American publisher for his last pre-war book, *Nous autres Français*. His usual sense of mission is also evident when he tells the religious that she is free to publish his letter and circulate it in any way she sees fit.

A final note in regard to a certain similarity with Léon Bloy is in order before leaving *Le Chemin de la Croix-des-Ames*. In a few of Bernanos' titles one detects a certain rapport with *Exégèse des lieux communs* wherein Bloy gave his own, inimitable exegeses of such overworked proverbs as "Business is business." When Bernanos chooses a topic such as "Hunger goes well with shame" and writes around it, using it as a point of departure, one easily recalls Bloy's earlier work. In the final analysis, this method may be considered a clever device of journalism; yet there is, perhaps, something a bit more substantial in the point of view being expressed by these two *visionnaires* than that expressed by the average journalist under an equally clever headline.

IX   Last Essays

The next volume to appear, *Last Essays*, was a compilation, prepared by Albert Béguin, of five lectures given by Bernanos in 1946 and 1947. Included is Bernanos' lecture at the Sorbonne in 1947 and his speech at the *Rencontres internationales* at Geneva in 1946.[7] The most important of these lectures for the student of Bernanos' thought, however, is the last one, "Our Friends, the Saints," given in Algeria, 1947, to a group of nuns of Père de Foucauld's order. Besides raising human freedom to the highest possible level—that of being necessary for a man to become holy —Bernanos also dwells on the mystery of the "communion of the saints," the mystery of who pays for whom and how God's justice works. Surely none of Bernanos' non-fictional pages, with the possible exception of the few pages of *Brother Martin*, are of any greater importance to understanding the author's profoundly Christian orientation towards life and the world in general.

X Le Crépuscule des vieux

Albert Béguin's next task, after bringing out *Last Essays*, was that of amassing texts dating from before the war—everything up to 1939. These were published under the title *Le Crépuscule des vieux* and include some unpublished pieces. This compilation is thus much more varied than *Last Essays*. Covering a thirty-year period, from 1909 to 1939, these articles touch upon purely literary topics and matters other than the immediate salvation of France and European civilization.

The editor divided this volume into five sections: (1) "Le Prince de ce monde," giving explanations made by Bernanos in 1926–27 concerning the meaning of his first novel; (2) "Sur la poésie," articles extending over the period 1928–1939 and dealing with poetry and poets; (3) "Lectures et spectacles," texts on various and varied subjects and covering the period 1909–1934; (4) "Primauté de la peur," giving another set of articles dating from 1928–1930 where literary and political judgments combine with thoughts on the nature of evil; (5) "L'Esprit de vieillesse," articles of the following two-year period (1931–1932), also covering a wide range of topics. These rather arbitrary divisions were made by Béguin and reflect certain of his own emphases. He has, let it be noted, provided an invaluable set of notes at the end of this volume.

The purely literary essays contained in *Le Crépuscule des vieux* are scattered throughout several sections and are of interest in that they give a student of that period an insight into Bernanos as a literary critic. There are articles on such poets as Cécile Sauvage, Eusèbe de Brémond d'Ars, Louis le Cardonnel and the Brazilian Jorge de Lima, while novelists such as Léon Daudet, Julien Green and Céline are treated.

The first section is of great value as a primary source in that it puts at the student's disposal Bernanos' views on himself and his first novel, *Under the Sun of Satan*. The contents of "Une vision catholique du réel" and "Satan et nous" should, ideally, be normal background reading for a reader attacking Bernanos' first novel in more than a cursory fashion.

XI Français, si vous saviez

The last volume of compilations, *Français, si vous saviez,* was published in 1961 by Antoine Travers and presents Bernanos' newspaper articles written after his return to France following the war. These articles thus cover the last four years of the author's life, 1945–1948.

As stated in the editor's front note, the texts reproduced in this book are those found in the newspapers from which they were taken, since the original manuscripts were not available. The editor justly remarks that this is especially regrettable since Bernanos complained bitterly about the cuts made in the texts of many of these articles. André Rousseaux, Bernanos' old friend and the well-known literary critic, has provided the introduction to this volume. The title, *Français si vous saviez,* comes from the last sentence of the initial article dated July 26, 1945, published in *La Bataille.*

In more than one respect this 378-page volume is a continuation of *Le Chemin de la Croix-des-Ames* and bears adequate witness to Bernanos' almost daily preoccupations the last years of his life. Since the author collaborated with a great number of newspapers, these articles form a sort of cross section of part of the French press of those early post-war years. Here, among a number of others, *La Bataille, L'Intrasigeant, Combat, Le Figaro* and *Carrefour* are represented, giving some idea of the general deployment of Bernanos' journalistic activity at the end of his life.

For those interested in the relations between François Mauriac and Bernanos, the editor has reproduced Mauriac's article on Bernanos printed in *Le Figaro* for June 23, 1946. In this way the reader can better understand Bernanos' answer, printed in *La Bataille* the following July 17. The oft-quoted comment Bernanos made concerning Mauriac's books where "carnal despair drips as though it were muddy water sweating from an underground wall" is repeated in Bernanos' article.[8] The conflict between Mauriac and Bernanos is noteworthy since both of them, in 1936, had been opposed to the "crusade" in Spain, representing the exceptional rather than the expected Catholic point of view.

This volume is, as is *Le Chemin de la Croix-des-Ames,* very rich and offers an invaluable insight into the deep anguish and horror Bernanos experienced upon returning to his country. And, in a higher sense, one also sees reflected here that personal passion which, in "God's sweet mercy," was given Bernanos to suffer at the end. How much more splendidly does the unconquerable hope of *The Carmelites* strike the reader when contrasted with the unhappy, disappointed tone of so many of these anguished articles.

Part III

Conclusion

I *Bernanos and Literature*

BERNANOS' present high standing among French writers of
the twentieth century seems to depend, and probably will
continue to depend, upon two works: *The Diary of a Country
Priest* and *The Carmelites*. Though the specialist and the occasional educated reader may rate *M. Ouine* as his real masterpiece
and though *Under the Sun of Satan* may, for sheer power, still
produce the most dramatic response in a reader, just as *Mouchette*
will always be admired for its purity of style, none of these novels
is likely to be the first title on the average reader's lips when he
thinks of Bernanos. Moreover, though a certain number of occasional readers will be attracted to read *A Crime*, or even *Joy*, few
will have the inclination to plunge into *L'Imposture* or *Night Is
Darkest*. Bernanos will thus remain for the general literate public
the author of two works.

That these two works are equally famous and of equal and
lasting appeal poses a problem, however, when it comes to classifying Bernanos. The reason for this problem is that one of these
principal works is a novel, the other a "play"—if one may call a
screen scenario that failed as a scenario a proper play. Regardless
of what it may be called, *The Carmelites* is definitely not a novel,
even to the extent that Faulkner's *Requiem for a Nun* is a novel
since the American master did give prose chapters in his work as
well as dramatic dialogue, something Bernanos did not do nor,
indeed, had any intention of doing.

What, then, is one to do if he wishes to regard Bernanos as a
novelist? Is one to ignore *The Carmelites*? Surely a certain scandal is caused by this work for the critics who are convinced that
the only valid approach to literature is by a study of *genre*. By
the sheer existence of *The Carmelites* all classification of Bernanos as a mere "novelist" becomes questionable since this work
accords perfectly with Bernanos' artistic vision and yet does not,
in any way, permit itself to be treated as a novel.

Because *The Carmelites* does so perfectly complement and
crown the whole of Bernanos' fiction, it surely therefore cannot
be ignored when one is trying to understand Bernanos' whole

artistic vision. To write a book—or even an article—on Bernanos'
novels and ignore *The Carmelites* is to present a truncated version of Bernanos' fictional world. Such distortion would apparently be aimed either at glorifying a cerebral notion that literature should be thus and so or else at demonstrating the critic's
own clever skills at fitting Bernanos' novels into his own private
scheme.

Bernanos himself would undoubtedly have enjoyed the scandal
his two most famous works pose for the critics since he was, while
being a very great writer and a very severe disciplinarian in
regard to the quality of his work, singularly scornful of the professional man of letters. For Bernanos, as he himself stated in the
preface to *A Diary of My Times,* his books were merely means of
revealing to certain chosen souls, for whom he believed he had
been born, his own understanding of the mysteries of God and
man. Is it therefore any wonder that he was not successful when
he tried to live and support his family by his pen alone?

It is imperative, nonetheless, that some comment be made upon
the case for viewing Bernanos as a novelist. He did, after all, lay
great store by his novels, saying even that "a novel is merciless"
when he was encouraging Vallery-Radot to write one.[1] He also
prided himself on being an humble disciple of the greatest French
master of the novel, Balzac. He also read Sir Walter Scott, Barbey
d'Aurevilly and Zola, to cite three others who distinguished themselves in this *genre.* The usual comment in regard to all this is
that Bernanos' real predecessor as a novelist is Barbey d'Aurevilly whose taste for things religious is, of course, quite obvious
and whose exotic predilection for what might be termed a "Catholic gothic" novel must surely have found in the young Bernanos
a not totally unsympathetic reader.

But the element of realism in Bernanos, that element of human
life which never abandons his most exotic passages—for example,
the incarnation of Satan in *Under the Sun of Satan* or the mystic
vision of Chantal de Clergerie in *Joy*—is never divorced completely from either the characters or the action. While Lucifer
tries his tricks and changes forms, Donissan remains profoundly
human, just as Chantal, with all her fatigue and all-too-human
despair also remains human as she views Christ's agony in the
garden. This simple, humble humanity would, of course, triumph

in the later novels of Bernanos since he struggled as much against the forms of exaggerated concepts of evil as against sublimity in things pertaining to God.

Such a note of human reality is unfortunately lacking in either Barbey's work or—strange as it may seem—also in that of Zola. Though completely opposed on many counts, these two authors, nonetheless, mutually failed to arrive at penetrating the personal secret of their characters' souls, nor did they, for that matter, ever succeed in breathing into their characters their own interior life as Bernanos did with all his major characters, whether sinner or saint.

Bernanos thus, besides approaching the world and man from dimensions other than those of Barbey and Zola, also surpasses both these writers in his powerful characterizations. In this we can discern the mark of the born novelist who follows in Balzac's footsteps. Though Balzac's creative gift was much greater than that of Bernanos, the diffuse spiritual quest of the master of *La Comédie Humaine* is not so likely to appeal to a reader. Balzac's spiritual experience seems to have failed to attain a level of universality which would make it of personal significance for any great number of readers. And it is here that Bernanos, though endowed with an inferior creative gift when compared with that of Balzac, did, as it were, possess the pearl of great price. His work's greatest appeal is in its spiritual validity which never fails to strike the reader sensitive to such a rare gift.

Thus, though Bernanos' quantity of production is far inferior to that of Balzac or even to that of Zola, there is a certain spiritual quality, an authenticity of inner experience which is hardly to be found elsewhere in modern French novels except, perhaps, in Léon Bloy's *La Femme Pauvre*. But much more joins Bloy and Bernanos than the *genre* of novel. Their personal experience of God and of the things of God renders them spiritual—and literary—brothers. Regardless of what they wrote or in what form they chose to write it, both masters continually bear witness to their respective experiences of the Absolute, just as did their other literary—and spiritual—brother, Charles Péguy.

Bloy, Péguy and Bernanos do indeed form both a spiritual and a literary current in the early twentieth century of which any of them, it may be assumed, would have been justly proud. They also defy any classification by *genre*. Once *genre* is dismissed, one is moreover free to see emerging a whole current in which one must include Ernest Hello, Bloy's friend and one of the literary —and spiritual—masters of Bernanos' adolescence. And, with the mention of the name of Hello, one launches upon the exploration of a rather rarified aspect of French literature, one that is usually ignored, that of prophecy, well established in the nineteenth century by Joseph de Maistre and Blanc de Saint-Bonnet. Yet perhaps it is as "prophets" that Bloy, Péguy and Bernanos are best classified: Christian prophets who wrote, among the three of them, in almost every literary form. Such a classification indeed transcends all idea of *genre* and emphasizes the heart of what the authors were saying rather than how and in what form they were saying it.

If placed, then, with Bloy and Péguy and classified as primarily a Christian prophet, is Bernanos thereby any nearer the much-vaunted masters of the "Catholic revival" of the twenties, Claudel and Mauriac? A negative answer seems imperative. Claudel surely did not share Bernanos' very salutary respect for the mystery of God's workings since he perennially tried to explain and elucidate these workings, charging his work with obvious symbolism piled upon obvious symbolism, reducing the most sacred and unspeakable mysteries of human suffering and expiation to matters for theatrical spectacle and poetic rhetoric. Bernanos' dislike for Claudel's work, in spite of his attachment to the letter Claudel wrote him in 1926 on publication of *Under the Sun of Satan*,[2] is surely to be found within that difference of Christian vision each author articulates. As for Mauriac, Bernanos also disliked his work and that unhealthy preoccupation with sex which causes its author to founder before arriving at any really deep spirituality.

Let it be added that while certain critics also attempt to view Julien Green as a novelist of Bernanos' stripe, yet here again, as in the case of Mauriac, one sees an author who has never been able to climb over a certain morbid adolescent preoccupation with sex. As a result, his whole work is rendered weaker and it is robbed of any really positive spirituality since the tumorous growth of the author's obsession saps its strength.

To mention minor writers, such as the contemporary Gilbert

Cesbron, or a writer of an earlier generation, such as Emile Baumann, seems equally without real relevance. By his great discipline and masterful power Bernanos wrote French literature in the grand tradition such as neither of these men have done. They cannot rise to the level of Bernanos because they are not in the same category to begin with.

Must one, then, despair of Bernanos' place, accepting the classification of "prophet" as being an unfortunate last resort? This classification does, after all, leave room for *The Carmelites* as well as the non-fiction. Though it may well be a "last resort," it is not certain that this classification is so unfortunate. One of the greatest names in French literature of the nineteenth century, Charles Baudelaire, did not disdain to speak as a prophet and perhaps, indeed, he is best classified as such.[3] And another great name in the nineteenth century was also equally prophetic: Arthur Rimbaud.[4] And, to confound those critics who favor *genre* as a means of classification, neither of these great poets disdained prose for uttering his prophecies. May it not be said, moreover, that the visions they enunciate in their prophecies are in complete accord with their "poetic" vision?

Perhaps, of course, the critics who insist on *genre* for the basis of classification would like to come forth with a new, all-inclusive *genre* which would be called "prophetic literature." Such a category, let it be admitted, however, would prove about as vague —and almost as all-inclusive—as a category called "moralistic literature." Would it not, therefore, appear desirable that all attempts at classification by *genre* be dropped in Bernanos' case if one wishes to arrive at some degree of understanding the man and what he was trying to say?

There is, let it be noted, one novelist's name which has frequently been linked to that of Bernanos, the Russian, Dostoyevsky. This great master, like Bernanos, understood the spiritual heights and depths of man and did not hesitate to show both, painting one as convincingly as the other. Both were also equally persuaded that man's heart is a battlefield where the forces of good and evil wage continual war. This teaching of the Christian desert Fathers both Bernanos and Dostoyevsky share in common. Perhaps this explains why Bernanos has, on occasion, been called the "French Dostoyevsky."

Bernanos would undoubtedly have considered this title a very high compliment since he loved the Russian's work. Their major difference is cultural, not spiritual. It lies primarily in the fact that Bernanos is definitely within the French literary tradition. Like Balzac, he gives long explanations of psychological motives while Dostoyevsky is content with implying such motives through his swift action and brilliant dialogue. Bernanos, moreover, tends to take a character and pursue him—often even in solitude—while Dostoyevsky tends to show his characters more in a definite social setting. Bernanos, let it be recalled, was brought up in a tradition where the classic theater consists of speech after speech analyzing feelings and principles, a theater which is singularly austere in its purity. It would seem inevitable that such an orientation would rub off on a novelist as deeply steeped in the totality of his own human heritage—not only his political and religious heritage, but also his literary heritage—as was Bernanos.

That Bernanos was a Catholic and Dostoyevsky an Orthodox Christian does not in any way really separate them. Bernanos' fury was as keen as Dostoyevsky's against that "jesuitical" principle of militant, totalitarian religion which would tell God what to do. Both share a profoundly Christian respect for the total mystery of the workings of God; both reveal their own personal veneration of that mystery. Indeed, Bloy and Péguy join with Bernanos in this emphasis on the mystery of God and of the way God works, recalling to students of "comparative literature" that if Dostoyevsky's approach to life is called Christian in an "Orthodox" way, as distinguished from a "Catholic" way, then surely Bloy, Péguy and Bernanos must also be called Christian in an "Orthodox" way.

This is not to intimate that any of these three writers would ever have appreciated being identified with a church which they would officially be expected to declare schismatic. Yet the fact remains that they are all too often regarded in their own Catholic fold as being "unorthodox" and a bit scandalous. It is equally true that Russian thinkers of the Paris immigration, such as the late Nicholas Berdaev and the contemporary thinker Paul Evdokimov, manifest an unusual and respectful interest for this current in twentieth-century French literature. Both of these Russians, moreover, show a very rare respect for Bloy. May it not be asked if the true ties, then, between this French current and that in which Dostoyevsky is found are not really yet to be established? It is the task which only a very great mind could undertake.

It is not, of course, the point of this book to go into these ties between Bernanos, Bloy, Péguy and Dostoyevsky, yet it can, perhaps, be briefly remarked that there is to be found in their works a consistent view of both God and man and the omnipresence of evil in this world. In his admirable book on Dostoyevsky, Berdaev speaks of Dostoyevsky's work as a part of the modern post-Renaissance world:

Therein man has a very different place from that given him by Dante or Shakespeare: he neither forms part of an unchangeable objective order nor exists on the surface of the earth, or of his own soul. Spiritual life is restored to him and he has found it in himself.[5]

Such a conclusion might well be drawn concerning the works of Bernanos and, in varying degrees, concerning the work of Bloy and Péguy. Indeed, the spiritual life of man was the constant preoccupation of all these writers as they pursued their respective artistic visions, hoping to reveal as they wrote the truth they glimpsed and thereby become worthy prophets of the living God.

Notes and References

Unless stated otherwise, all books in these notes and references were published in Paris.

In addition, the following abbreviations will be used:

ANG   William Bush, *L'Angoisse du Mystère, Essai sur Bernanos et M. Ouine,* Minard, 1966.

BUL   *Bulletin de la Société des Amis de Georges Bernanos.* Bulletin trimestriel du n° 1 (décembre 1949) au n° 4 (juin 1950); bulletin périodique à partir du n° 5 (Noël 1950).

CLUB   *M. Ouine,* Première édition intégrale conforme au manuscrit et comportant de nombreuses pages inédites. Texte établi par Albert Béguin. Suivi d'un article, "Histoire d'un roman," par Albert Béguin. Club des Libraires de France, 1955.

GB   *Georges Bernanos,* Essais et Témoignages réunis par Albert Béguin, Les Cahiers du Rhône, Le Baconnière, Neuchatel, and Seuil, 1949.

LM   Albert Béguin, *Bernanos par lui-même,* Images et textes inédits présentés par Albert Béguin, Seuil, 1954.

OE   Geogres Bernanos, *Oeuvres romanesques suivies de Dialogues des Carmélites* (Bibliothèque de la Pléiade), Préface par Gaëton Picon, Texte et variantes établis par Albert Béguin, Notes par Michel Estève, Gallimard, 1961.

SE   William Bush, *Souffrance et Expiation dans la Pensée de Bernanos,* Minard, 1962.

Part I

1. H. Tribout de Morembert, "Les Origines Lorraines de G. Bernanos," BUL 21.
2. *Ibid.*
3. *Ibid.*
4. *Ibid.*
5. Information relating to how Hermance Moreau came to Paris and how Emile Bernanos came to set himself up in business was con-

veyed to the author in a conversation with Abbé Daniel Pezeril in 1957.

6. GB, p. 349.

7. "Nos Amis les Saints" in *La Liberté pour quoi faire?*

8. LM, p. 34.

9. GB, pp. 250–253.

10. These letters were included in OE and provide an excellent primary source for understanding the nature of Bernanos' interior life (OE, pp. 1723–1738).

11. In 1957 the author had the opportunity to visit in Pas-de-Calais and converse with a number of people who had known the young Bernanos. The highlight of this literary pilgrimage was the warm blessing bestowed upon the author by Abbé Louis Merlin, Bernanos' nonagenarian former professor of rhetoric at the Collège Sainte-Marie at Aire-sur-Lys.

12. D. W. Brogan, *The Development of Modern France*, Hamish Hamilton (London: 1953), p. 370.

13. Bernanos' activities may be referred to in the following issues of the *Action française:* Jan. 14, 1909; Feb. 9, 1909; Mar. 10, 1909; Mar. 16, 17, 1909; Oct. 20, 1909; Mar. 28, 1912; June 29, 1912.

14. The place of esteem in which Henri Tilliette was held by his *Camelots* brothers in arms may be surmised from the letter Michel Estève has reproduced in *Bernanos*, "La Bibliothèque Idéale," Gallimard, 1965, p. 49.

15. *L'Avant-Garde de Normandie*, Feb. 8, 1914.

16. Madame Georges Bernanos related this information to the author in 1957, as well as the fact that it was also she who had introduced her husband, at the same time, to Dostoyevsky.

17. BUL 2-3, pp. 20–21.

18. BUL 1, Article by Robert Vallery-Radot, "Souvenirs d'un Ami."

19. OE, p. 1757.

20. BUL 51–52, p. 8.

21. Henry Jamet. See Jamet's book, *Un Autre Bernanos*, Vitte (Lyon: 1959), 115 pp., for a view of the man which must have been all too common among most of Bernanos' well-meaning friends.

22. GB, p. 350.

23. *Action française*, Apr. 26, 1926.

24. BUL 53-54, p. 7.

25. OE, p. 1771.

26. Jean de Fabrègues, *Bernanos tel qu'il était*, Mame, 1964, p. 100.

27. OE, p. 1854.

28. See BUL 17–20 which gives details of this polemic and of Bernanos' collaboration with *Le Figaro* at this time.

29. As Albert Béguin pointed out in CLUB (p. 294), Bernanos felt sure at this time that he would complete the novel in a few months and thus in June, 1933, authorized Plon to take subscriptions for a deluxe edition of his "great novel." The unhappy subscribers were obliged to wait thirteen years before the novel appeared in any form in France.

30. ANG, pp. 15–27.

31. OE, p. 1855.

32. GB, p. 348.

33. When *Un mauvais rêve* (*Night Is Darkest*) was first published by Albert Béguin in *La Table Ronde* the founder of the Bernanos Society provided an invaluable introduction to this work and to this whole period of Bernanos' life. See his article "Bernanos au travail," *La Table Ronde*, 34, Oct. 1950, pp. 9–25.

34. ANG, pp. 25–27.

35. OE, p. 1852.

36. This anecdote was related to the author in July, 1957, by Madame Georges Bernanos.

37. See BUL 4.

38. *Le Chemin de la Croix-des-Ames* was subsequently published in a single volume after the war.

39. In a conversation in 1959 with Albert Béguin's successor at *Esprit* the author had pointed out to him the great difference the young men of the Resistance felt there was between the Bernanos who had inspired them with his writings during the war and the Bernanos who harangued them at the Sorbonne after the war. As Bernanos might himself have said, it was a question of disappointing a great love.

40. Thomas Molnar, *Bernanos, His Political Thought and Prophecy*, Sheed and Ward (New York, 1960), p. 157.

41. GB, p. 309.

42. *Idem.*, p. 315.

43. *La Liberté pour quoi faire?*, "Nos Amis les Saints."

44. GB, p. 355.

45. See *L'Herne*, no. 2, where the author has tried to elucidate the spiritual ties between Bernanos and his two favorite saints, Thérèse of Lisieux and Jeanne d'Arc.

46. GB, p. 355.

47. A photograph of these pages has been reproduced in GB, plates XXIII and XXIV.

Part II

Chapter 1

1. Albert Béguin in LM underlined this theme. Since it has been further studied by other students of Bernanos: Marie-Agnès Fragnière, *Bernanos fidèle à l'enfant*, Editions universitaires (Fribourg: 1963), 155 pp.; Yves Bridel, *L'Esprit de l'enfance dans l'Oeuvre romanesque de Georges Bernanos*, Minard, 1966, 272 pp.; SE pp. 103–125, a chapter also published in *Revue des Lettres Modernes*, Autumn 1960, pp. 333–355 (*Etudes bernanosiennes* no. 1, pp. 109–131).

2. Even Albert Béguin in LM tends to defend this idea that the priest is the central figure in Bernanos' novels. See LM, pp. 68–83.

3. See Guy Gaucher, *Le Thème de la Mort dans les Romans de Bernanos*, Lettres Modernes, 1955.

4. SE, pp. 103–125.

5. Hans Urs von Balthazar, *Bernanos*, Verlag Jacob Hegner (Köln & Olten: 1954), translated into French by Maurice de Gandillac as *Le Chrétien Bernanos*, Seuil, 1956. The French edition suppresses the 22 pages of biography of the original German text.

6. See SE.

7. The character of the curé of Torcy in *Diary of a Country Priest* is not only avowedly Flemish, but also typical of one side of Bernanos' own personal spirituality. A similar phenomenon of identification can be seen in the character of Sr. Constance in *The Carmélites*.

8. While it is true that Bernanos was apparently happy at the Jesuit *collège* on the rue de Vaugirard where he was a day student only, he was not happy as a boarding student at Notre-Dame-des-Champs. Albert Béguin in LM confused these two institutions since he assumed that Bernanos' remarks against the Jesuit system were aimed at the Vaugirard school. It is understandable, however, that such a mistake could occur since the superior of Notre-Dame-des-Champs was also a Jesuit and no doubt ran his school according to the severity of Jesuit discipline. He it was who suggested to Bernanos' parents that their son be sent to a commercial school.

9. OE, p. 237: Connaître pour détruire, et renouveler dans la destruction sa connaissance et son désir—ô soleil de Satan!—désir du néant recherché pour lui-même, abominable effusion du coeur!

10. Genesis III: 5.

11. See SE, pp. 33–59, where a whole chapter is devoted to the mediocre and *imbéciles* in Bernanos' thought.

12. OE, p. 681. Car à présent, l'idée, la certitude de son impuissance était devenue le centre éblouissant de sa joie.

Chapter 2

1. *Le Panache.*
2. See GB, p. 285.
3. See OE, p. 1755, note 1 for p. 15 and OE, p. 1756, note 1 for
p. 39.

Chapter 3

1. On pilgrimage to Ars in 1956, the author has verified this startling detail for himself. But even more startling, though not so publi-
cized, are the blood-stained, nail-studded belts of penance worn by
the holy peasant. Bernanos, true to his model, incorporated such instru-
ments of self-torture into his novel.
2. OE, p. 1847.
3. *Action française,* Apr. 26, 1926.
4. OE, p. 237. See Note 9 for Chapter 1, Part II above.
5. *Ibid.* (...) ce délire de la connaissance qui perdit la mère des
hommes, droite et pensive, au seuil du Bien et du Mal.
6. This statement is best known to modern readers from T. S. Eliot's
use of it at the end of the *Four Quartets,* Dame Julian's *Revelations of
Divine Love* not being quite as widely circulated among the literate
public!
7. The text of this letter has been printed in OE, pp. 1763–64 and
in GB, pp. 64–66. A photographic reproduction of it will be found in
LM, pp. 156–157.

Chapter 4

1. Bernanos was not very happy about this decision. See OE, p.
1766.
2. This volume is available in translation and in more than one
edition from the Carmel of Lisieux, Calvados, France. The most au-
thoritative and reliable edition is the one entitled: *Sainte Thérèse de
l'Enfant Jésus, Manuscrits autobiographiques,* Carmel de Lisieux, 1957,
349 pp. The edition Bernanos would have known would have been
the one entitled *Histoire d'une Ame* which suffered from certain altera-
tions made by the well-meaning nuns. Of especial interest for understanding the basis of Bernanos' theme of "impotence" in spirituality is
the saint's "Acte d'offrande à l'Amour Miséricordieux" found in the
Manuscrits autobiographiques on pp. 318–320.
3. See Guy Gaucher, "Bernanos et Sainte Thérèse de l'Enfant Jésus," *Revue des Lettres Modernes* no. 56–57, Autumn, 1960, pp.
225–268 (*Etudes bernanosiennes* no. 1, pp. 3–44).

4. OE, p. 681. See Note 12 for Chapter 1, Part II above.

5. See the author's analysis of this evolution of Bernanos' ideas on expiation in SE pp. 18–29.

6. La Démission de la France.

Chapter 5

1. Albert Béguin, "Bernanos au Travail," *La Table Ronde*, no. 34, Oct., 1950, pp. 9–25.

2. *Ibid.*

3. Béguin speaks of ties between Cénabre, Ganse, Ouine and Bernanos in LM, p. 7. See also ANG, pp. 207–211 where the author has tried to arrive at further conclusions in regard to this.

4. See BUL 35–36, pp. 1–4.

5. OE, p. 1803.

Chapter 6

1. BUL 35–36, pp. 1–4.

2. See Chapter 5 above.

3. OE, p. 1846.

4. *Idem.*, p. 1847.

5. *Ibid.*

6. OE, p. 1258. Il est plus facile que l'on croit de se haïr. La grâce est de s'oublier. Mais si tout orgueil était mort en nous, la grâce des grâces serait de s'aimer humblement soi-même, comme n'importe lequel des membres souffrants de Jésus-Christ.

7. *La Liberté pour quoi faire?*, p. 282.

8. OE, p. 1852.

Chapter 7

1. See ANG.

2. CLUB.

3. The interpretation given by the author in ANG is but a beginning, though seven years of constant reflection upon the significance of *M. Ouine* went into that essay. *M. Ouine,* like Péguy's *Eve*, is one of the true masterpieces of this century whose preference for current fads can only recall those preferences of the late nineteenth century for Bourget instead of the genial Bloy.

4. Albert Béguin himself launched this idea in LM, p. 78, and it has been repeated many times since.

5. The author in his thesis for the Sorbonne (SE) first attempted to express this more balanced view of M. Ouine (SE, pp. 89–94).

6. OE, p. 1557. S'il n'y avait rien, je serais quelque chose, bonne ou mauvaise. C'est moi qui ne suis rien.

7. OE, p. 1362.

8. Luke I: 38.

9. CLUB, p. 289.

Chapter 8

1. Sister Meredith Murray, O.P., has given a very thorough presentation of the facts concerning the ties between the two authors in her book, *La Genèse de DIALOGUES DES CARMELITES*, an indispensable reference for this subject (Seuil, 1963, 175 pp.).

2. See the article by Abbé Daniel Pezeril, "Le film du P. Bruckberger est-il fidèle à Bernanos?", BUL 39–40.

3. Two French books on this historic execution were brought out as a result of Bernanos' play, one of them a very imposing scholarly work, the other a short, popular one: Père Bruno de Jésus-Marie, *Le Sang du Carmel ou la véritable Passion des Seize Carmélites de Compiègne*, Plon, 1954, 559 pp.; Claude Saint-Yves, *Le vrai Dialogues des Carmélites*, Le Centurion, 1955, 125 pp.

4. OE, p. 1585. Qui s'aveugle volontairement sur le prochain, sous prétexte de charité, ne fait souvent rien autre chose que de briser le miroir afin de ne pas se voir dedans.

5. OE, p. 1584. Car on compte un certain nombre de vraies religieuses, mais bien davantage de médiocres et d'insipides.

Chapter 9

1. *Les Enfants Humiliés*, Gallimard, 1949, p. 205.

2. Henri Massis was editor-in-chief of this review published by Plon and directed by Jacques Bainville.

3. LM, pp. 95–96.

4. *Le Mystère de l'Eglise*, Editions du Cerf, 1917.

5. *Ibid.*, p. 134. Here, however, the religious states "*L'on dit* qu'il faut savoir souffrir etc.," which causes one to wonder if the idea were originally his. In any case, it was he who transmitted it to Bernanos as attested in BUL 24–25, p. 7.

6. GB, p. 350.

7. A short recording of Bernanos' voice (Philips A 76–719 R) was made during his lecture at Geneva, and the text of this recording is thus contained within that speech in this volume. Portions of this first recording have more recently been included in a larger recording entitled, "*Les Ecrivains du XXe siècle* (Philips V32–A [30]).

8. *Français, si vous saviez*, Gallimard, 1961, p. 175. (...) le déses-

poir charnel transpire comme une eau boueuse au mur d'un souter-
rain (...).

Part III

1. BUL 53–54, p. 8. Letter dated Dec. 28, 1926.
2. See note 7 for Chapter 3, Part II above.
3. See Charles Baudelaire, *Oeuvres Complètes*, Bibliothèque de la
Pléiade, Gallimard, 1961, pp. 1262–1265. This conclusion to the notes,
generally entitled "Fusées," surely lays the poet's heart as bare as any
passage in *"Mon coeur mis à nu."*
4. See Arthur Rimbaud's *Une Saison en Enfer* and *Les Illumina-
tions.*
5. Nicholas Berdyaev, *Dostoyevsky*, translated by Donald Attwater,
Meridian Books (New York: 1957), pp. 49–50.

Annotated Bibliography

PRIMARY SOURCES

All books were published in Paris, unless otherwise stated. Principal editions only are listed here. Publication in periodicals is indicated within parentheses.

Bernanos' Fiction

"Madame Dargent"
    (1922: *La Revue hebdomadaire*)
    1955: Plon, in *Dialogue d'ombres*.
    1961: Gallimard, in *Oeuvres romanesques*.

Sous le Soleil de Satan
    1926: Plon.
    1961: Gallimard, in *Oeuvres romanesques*.

In English
The Star of Satan, trans. by Veronica Lukas, John Lane (London: 1927).
The Star of Satan, trans. by Pamela Morris, Macmillan (New York: 1940). This same translation was published in England as *Star of Satan*, John Lane (London: 1940).
Under the Sun of Satan, trans. by Harry L. Binsse, Pantheon (New York: 1949).

L'Imposture
    1927: Plon.
    1961: Gallimard, in *Oeuvres romanesques*.
"Une nuit"
    (1928: *La Revue hebdomadaire*)
    1928: Cité des livres.
    1955: Plon, in *Dialogues d'ombres*.
    1961: Gallimard, in *Oeuvres romanesques*.
"Dialogue d'ombres"
    (1928: *Nouvelle Revue Française*)
    1928: Cité des livres.

1955: Plon in *Dialogue d'ombres*. This collection, besides the title story, includes "Madame Dargent," "Une nuit" and four of the early fictional attempts from 1913: "Virginie," "La Muette," "La Tombe refermée" and "La Mort avantageuse du chevalier de Lorges." All these were reprinted in 1961 in Gallimard's *Oeuvres romanesques*.

1961: Gallimard, in *Oeuvres romanesques*.

La Joie

(1928: *La Revue universelle*)

1929: Plon.

1954: Club du meilleur livre (édition critique d'Albert Béguin).

1961: Gallimard, in *Oeuvres romanesques*.

In English
Joy, trans. by Louise Varese, Pantheon (New York: 1946); Bodley Head (London: 1948).

Un Crime

1935: Plon.

1961: Gallimard, in *Oeuvres romanesques*.

In English
The Crime, trans. by Anne Green, R. Hale & Co. (London: 1936). This same translation was published in the United States as *A Crime*, E. P. Dutton (New York: 1936).

Journal d'un curé de campagne

(1935–36: *La Revue hebdomadaire*)

1936: Plon.

Gallimard, in *Oeuvres romanesques*.

1964: Le livre de poche "Université" (étude et notes de Michel Estève).

In English
Diary of a Country Priest, trans. by Pamela Morris, Boriswood (London: 1937). This same translation was published in the United States under the same title in 1954 by Image Books, reprinted in England by Collins in 1956.

Nouvelle histoire de Mouchette

1937: Plon.

1961: Gallimard, in *Oeuvres romanesques*.

In English
Mouchette, trans. by J. C. Whitehouse, Holt, Rinehart and Winston
    (New York: 1966).
M. Ouine
    1943:   Atlantica (Rio de Janeiro).
    1946:   Plon.
    1955:   Club des Libraires de France (édition critique d'Albert
            Béguin).
    1961:   Gallimard, in *Oeuvres romanesques*. This text is that
            established by Béguin in the 1955 edition.

In English
The Open Mind, trans. by Geoffry Dunlop, John Lane (London:
    1945).

Un mauvais rêve
    (1950:   *La Table Ronde*)
    1950:   Plon. Both a normal and a critical edition were issued at
            the same time, both prepared by Albert Béguin.
    1961:   Gallimard, in *Oeuvres romanesques*.

In English
Night Is Darkest, trans. by W. J. Strachan, Bodley Head (London:
    1953).

Dialogues des Carmélites
    1949:   La Baconnière (Neuchâtel) and Seuil.
    1961:   Gallimard, in *Oeuvres romanesques*.

In English
The Fearless Heart, trans. by Michel Legat, Bodley Head (London:
    1952). The same translation was published in the United States
    by the Newman Press (Westminster, Md.: 1952).
The Carmelites, trans. by G. Hopkins, Collins (London: 1961).

Bernanos' Non-fiction

Saint Dominique
    (1926:   *La Revue universelle*)
    1927:   La Tour d'Ivoire.
    1939:   Gallimard (Collection catholique).
Jeanne, relapse et sainte
    (1929:   *La Revue hebdomadaire*)
    1934:   Plon.

In English
Sanctity Will Out, An Essay on St. Joan, trans. by R. Batchelor, Sheed and Ward (London: 1947).

La Grande peur des bien-pensants
    1931:   Grasset.
Les Grands cimetières sous la lune
    1938:   Plon.

In English
A Diary of My Times, trans. by Pamela Morris, Boriswood (London: 1938), Macmillan (New York: 1938).

Scandale de la vérité
    1939:   Gallimard.

Nous autres Français
    1939:   Gallimard.
Lettre aux Anglais
    1942:   Atlantica (Rio de Janeiro).
    1944:   Atlantica (Rio de Janeiro) and Charlot (Algiers).
    1946:   Gallimard.

In English
Plea for Liberty, Letters to the English, the Americans, the Europeans, trans. by Harry Lorin Binsse, Pantheon (New York: 1944). In England *Plea for Liberty,* trans. by Harry Lorin Binsse and Ruth Bethell, was published by Dennis Dobson (London: 1945).

Ecrits de combat
    1942–1944:   Imprimerie du Journal *La Syrie et l'Orient* (Beirut).
Le Chemin de la Croix-des-Ames
    1943–1945:   Atlantica (Rio de Janeiro), 4 volumes.
    1948:   Gallimard.

La France contre les robots
    1944:   Atlantica (Rio de Janeiro).
    1947:   Laffont.
    1955:   Club français du livre (édition critique d'Albert Béguin).

In English
Tradition of Freedom, translator anonymous, Dennis Dobson (London: 1950).

Réflexions sur le cas de conscience français
> 1945:   Editions de la revue Fontaine (Algiers). Text of a lecture
> given in Rio de Janeiro in 1943.

Les Enfants humiliés
> 1949:   Gallimard.

In English

Selections were published by *Months* in two issues in 1949 as "Dog's
life" and "Poor Fools."

"Frère Martin"
> (1951:   *Esprit*)

In English

"Brother Martin," trans. by Edwin W. Geissman in *Cross Currents*,
vol. II, summer (1952).

La Liberté pour quoi faire?
> 1953:   Gallimard. Lectures given in 1946–1947.

In English

Last Essays, trans. by Joan and Barry Ulanov, Henry Regnery (Chi-
cago: 1955).

Le Crépuscule des vieux
> 1956:   Gallimard. Compilation of various texts covering 1909–
> 1939.

Français, si vous saviez
> 1961:   Gallimard. Articles for 1945–1948.

Collected works

Oeuvres de Bernanos, La Palatine (Geneva: 1947), 6 vols. Includes all
the fiction (Plon text for *M. Ouine*) with the exception of *Un
mauvais rêve* and early fiction. Also included are the following
works of non-fiction: *Saint Dominique, Jeanne, relapse et sainte*,
and *Les Grands cimetières sous la lune*.

Romans, Gallimard (1959).

Oeuvres romanesques, suivies de *Dialogues des Carmélites*, Gallimard
(1961), Bibliothèque de la Pléiade. Péface de Gaëtan Picon.
Texte établi par A. Béguin. Biographie et notes par Michel Estève. This volume, since its publication, is the standard one. The

early fiction as well as the youthful letters of Bernanos to Abbé Lagrange are included. The notes are rich with a wealth of relevant letters and texts.

Prefaces Written by Bernanos

RAYMOND CHRISTOFLOUR, *Louis Le Cardonnel, pèlerin de l'invisible,* Plon (1938). Préface de Georges Bernanos.

RAYMOND LÉPOLD BRUCKBERGER, O.P., *Si grande peine . . .,* Gallimard (1945). Avertissement par P. Guillain de Benouville, Georges Bernanos.

LUC ESTANG, *Présence de Bernanos,* Plon (1947). Préface de Georges Bernanos: "Dans l'amitié de Léon Bloy." This preface is an important text.

PAUL FRONVILLE, *Hors de l'intelligence, pas de salut,* R. Lacoste (1949). Lettre-préface de Georges Bernanos.

VINCENT MONTEIRO, *Mon onde était trop courte pour toi (1939-41),* Seghers (1956). Lettre-préface de Georges Bernanos.

Other Primary Sources

Other major primary sources where texts by Bernanos may be found include the following:

BULLETIN de la Société des Amis de Georges Bernanos of which 58 numbers have appeared since its first issue in 1949.

Georges Bernanos, Essais et témoignages réunis par Albert Béguin, La Baconnière (Neuchatel) and Seuil (1949).

ALBERT BEGUIN, *Bernanos par lui-même,* Seuil (1954).

L'Herne, no 2, 1962. A whole issue devoted to Bernanos, including some previously unpublished texts by Bernanos.

"Si vous cessiez de vous hair . . .," *Esprit,* July–August, 1966. This is a heretofore unpublished text giving a scene from Chapter XVI of *M. Ouine* which Bernanos pushed aside and later rewrote. This fair version was prepared by Abbé Daniel Pezeril from a very rough original and is open to question on certain details.

Réaction, Paris, May, 1931. A whole issue of a young review devoted to Bernanos.

SECONDARY SOURCES

Books in English

GERDA BLUMENTHAL, *The Poetic Imagination of Georges Bernanos,*

The Johns Hopkins Press (Baltimore: 1965). This literary study of the novels and two of the short stories aims at supporting its author's basic dualism, thus missing the essential unity in Bernanos.

PETER HEBBLETHWAITE, S. J., *Bernanos, An Introduction,* Bowes and Bowes (London: 1965), "Studies in Modern European Literature and Thought." This little book aims at introducing Bernanos to an English public and thus brings in various references to English authors. The author understands and respects Bernanos and conveys these sentiments to the reader in a persuasive manner.

THOMAS MOLNAR, *Bernanos, His Political Thought and Prophecy,* Sheed and Ward (New York: 1960). This first book in English on Bernanos is helpful in giving political background for one encountering Bernanos for the first time, but it should not be relied upon when its author tries to deal with the fiction or with the deeper implications of Bernanos' thought—political or otherwise.

Books in French

Unless otherwise stated, all books were published in Paris.

ALBERT BÉGUIN, *Bernanos par lui-même,* Seuil (1954). This little volume is still the best introduction available both to the man and to his thought, though its author died 1957 and much work has been done since. But the hypotheses found in this book are still, for the most part, to be explored.

————, *Georges Bernanos,* Essais et témoignages réunis par Albert Béguin, La Baconnière (Neuchatel), and Seuil (1949). An invaluable source of information giving letters, memories of friends, literary and political history and the very beautiful account of Bernanos' death by Abbé Pezeril.

JOSEPH BOLY, *Dialogues des Carmelites, étude et analyse,* Editions de l'Ecole (1960). An aid for students and classroom study of the work.

YVES BRIDEL, *L'Esprit d'enfance dans l'oeuvre romanesque de Georges Bernanos,* Minard (1966). A very thoroughgoing thematic study which might serve as an introduction.

WILLIAM BUSH, *L'Agoisse du Mystère, Essai sur Bernanos et M. OUINE,* Minard (1966). An introduction to the richness of Bernanos' "great novel."

————, *Souffrance et Expiation dans la Pensée de Bernanos,* Minard (1962). A thematic study giving especial emphasis to Bernanos' spiritual evolution.

Louis Chaigne, *Georges Bernanos,* Editions Universitaires (1954). Several errors of fact mar what might have been a useful short introduction.

Henri Deblüe, *Les Romans de Georges Bernanos ou le défi du rêve,* La Baconnière (Neuchatel: 1965). A major contribution by its imposing size, this literary analysis nonetheless bypasses all question of chronology and of the evolution of the author, submitting his novels to an *a priori* pattern.

Luc Estang, *Présence de Bernanos,* Plon (1947). Written during Bernano's lifetime by a young friend and given a very important preface by Bernanos, this serious study should be carefully considered though it may be, in some ways, rather dated. In any case the preface, "Dans l'amitié de Léon Bloy," is one of Bernanos' very important short pieces, establishing a basis for rapport between him and Bloy.

Michel Estève, *Bernanos,* La Bibliothèque Idéale, Gallimard (1965). A very useful general introduction not only to Bernanos and his work, but also to the criticism. Very helpful summaries of Bernanos' books are given.

———, *Le Sens de l'amour dans les romans de Bernanos,* Minard (1959). This thematic study shows love as the motivating power behind Bernanos' characters who react either to love, or to being deprived of it.

Jean de Fabrègues, *Bernanos tel qu'il était,* Mame (1964). Written by a young friend of Bernanos who found in him inspiration during his youth, this book is important as a personal witness and is especially valuable when dealing with the years the author was associated with Bernanos.

Marie-Agnès Fragnière, *Bernanos fidèle à l'enfant,* Editions Universitaires (Fribourg: 1964). A short study on the theme of childhood and its role in Bernanos' work.

Guy Gaucher, *Le Thème de la Mort dans les romans de Bernanos,* Minard (1955). A short but very solid thematic study. Contains some unpublished letters of Bernanos.

———, *Georges Bernanos ou l'invincible espérance,* Plon (1962). A short and rather personal meditation on the spiritual implications of Bernanos. This little volume has been the center of much dispute. Praised by some and damned by others, it is not likely ever to appeal to the purely literary interest.

Jessie Lynn Gillespie, *Le Tragique dans l'oeuvre de Georges Bernanos,* Droz (Geneva) and Minard (1960). Using Gouhier's ideas on tragedy, the author turns over every conceivable situation with patient thoroughness without, however, having necessarily illuminated Bernanos himself.

BERNARD HALDA, *Bernanos, Le Scandale de croire,* Editions du Centurion (1965). A general introduction to the man and his work, a bit too simple in its understanding of evil in Bernanos.

HENRY JAMET, *Un autre Bernanos,* Vitte (Lyon: 1959). A short, very personal interpretation of Bernanos by one of his former friends whose basic lack of sympathy and understanding for Bernanos is evident throughout.

FRÉDÉRIC LEFÈVRE, *Georges Bernanos,* La Tour d'Ivoire (1926). The first book written on Bernanos at a moment when he had just been launched.

SISTER MARIE-CELESTE, *Le Sens de l'agonie dans l'oeuvre de Georges Bernanos,* P. Lethielleux (1961). An introduction to Bernanos as much as a thematic study, this study touches upon one of the basic psychological conditions of the man and his work without, however, arriving at any new conclusions.

PIERRE MAUBREY, *L'Expression de la passion intérieure dans le style de Bernanos romancier,* The Catholic University of America Press (Washington: 1959). A study giving its author an opportunity to scrutinize words and names in Bernanos and apply his imagination thereto in a sometimes rather arbitrary manner.

LÉA MOCH, *La Sainteté dans les romans de Bernanos,* Les Belles-Lettres (Lyon: 1962). A very short essay which never gets beyond the level of a general introduction to Bernanos. Sanctity, one of the key ideas in Bernanos' personal and literary orientation, is not studied, a very commonplace conception of it having been accepted by the author.

SISTER MEREDITH MURRAY, O.P., *La Genèse de "Dialogues des Carmélites,"* Seuil (1963). An indispensable study containing a wealth of facts both on Gertrude von le Fort and Bernanos.

GAËTAN PICON, *Georges Bernanos,* Robert Marin (1948). An early book written with sympathy by a purely literary critic.

JEAN SCHEIDEGGER, *Georges Bernanos romancier,* Attinger (Neuchatel: 1956). A discussion of the novelist's techniques regarding the world of Bernanos, with emphasis on the darker side.

HANS URS VON BALTHAZAR, *Le Chrétien Bernanos* (traduit de l'allemand par Maurice de Gandillac), Seuil (1956). This translation of the noted German-Swiss theologian's monumental volume on Bernanos remains, to date, the most imposing study consecrated to Bernanos. While very complete in one sense, it still misses the essentials, having been conceived around a given context: the seven Sacraments. Such an arbitrary division of Bernanos' world can only lead to arbitrary conclusions. The French translation surpressed the biographical section in the original German published by Hegner Verlag (Cologne & Olten: 1954).

Reviews Devoted to Bernanos

BULLETIN *de la Société des Amis de Georges Bernanos,* (distributed by M. J. Minard, 73 rue de Cardinal-Lemoine, Paris V) of which 58 numbers have appeared since its first issue in 1949.

"Etudes bernanosiennes," periodic issues of *La Revue des Lettres Modernes* devoted exclusively to Bernanos and edited by Michel Estève. Since its first number in 1960 seven issues have appeared.

DATE DUE

GAYLORD			PRINTED IN U.S.A.